Student Workbook to Accompany Crisis Communications

Student Workbook to Accompany Crisis Communications

A Casebook Approach
Fourth Edition

Kathleen Fearn-Banks
University of Washington

Routledge
Taylor & Francis Group

NEW YORK AND LONDON

First edition published 1996
by Lawrence Erlbaum Associates Inc.

Second edition 2002
by Lawrence Erlbaum Associates Inc.

Third edition 2008
by Routledge

This edition published 2011
by Routledge
711 Third Avenue, New York, NY 10017

Simultaneously published in the UK
by Routledge
2 Park Square, Milton Park, Abingdon, Oxon OX14 4RN

Routledge is an imprint of the Taylor & Francis Group, an informa business

© 2011 Taylor & Francis

The right of Kathleen Fearn-Banks to be identified as author of this work
has been asserted by her in accordance with sections 77 and 78 of the
Copyright, Designs and Patents Act 1988.

Typeset in Sabon and Gill Sans by
Florence Production Ltd, Stoodleigh, Devon

ISBN13: 978–0-415–88177–7 (pbk)

Contents

Preface

This workbook supplements the fourth edition of *Crisis Communications: A Casebook Approach*.

Instructors of crisis communications courses and courses including crisis communications will use it in various ways. In each chapter, there are suggestions for activities/exercises and discussion topics. Some have small sections of supplementary reading and lists of words and terms one should know after reading the chapter.

Chapter 15, The Crisis Communications Plan, is a step-by-step process for developing the crisis communications plan. Actual plans are located in the appendices of the textbook. Persons and groups working independently to develop crisis communications plans should find this chapter helpful.

Acknowledgments

We thank the following students at the University of Washington for their assistance: Melissa Ferrer, Casandra Grob, Victoria Ju, Katie McElroy, Tram Nguyen, Zoe Saurs, and Kristin Scheidegger.

Chapter 1

Crisis Communications Today

The tragedies of September 11 marked a turning point in the perception of the word "crisis," especially for people in the United States who had never experienced such an attack on their own soil. The attacks were also a turning point in the perceptions of crisis management and crisis communications.

A crisis management/communications plan saved the lives of numerous people in the World Trade Center (WTC) on that fateful day. Rick Rescola was head of security for Morgan Stanley, which occupied 40 floors in one of the WTC towers. After the 1993 terrorist attack on the WTC, Rescola formed a crisis management team to try to avert an attack or to help employees survive another attack. The team members were in agreement that another attack would occur, and that it would probably occur at the WTC because of the symbolism of the towers being the tallest in the United States.

Team Rescola, as it was called, determined that the next attack would not be a ground attack, because the garage was protected after the 1993 incident. They even took a test flight around the buildings and predicted the attack would be by air.

Crisis communications was necessary to convince employees and managers that preparations needed to be made and that training for evacuation was necessary, and to explain how it would be done. Subsequently, there were drills. Rescola had lighting put in the stairways, and every person knew where the stairways were.

When the planes struck, WTC security advised all persons that it was safer to stay in the building. Rescola and his team began to evacuate employees. A glitch occurred, in that one of the stairways was blocked by debris. Visibility was hampered either by smoke or darkness or both. Survivors and some of Rescola's team members, consultants who were not in the building at the time, told the History Channel that team Rescola went to each floor and yelled, "Is anyone here?" If so, they led them out by alternate stairways. They say the team saved 95 percent of the total number of Morgan Stanley employees.

However, there was not enough time for them to reach every floor. Rescola and some of his team members died when the buildings collapsed. His wife said, when she saw the buildings go down on television, she knew her husband was there still trying to get everyone out.

Activities

1. Look up funds raised by the American Red Cross in recent disasters, locally, nationally, and internationally. Is there a way to determine how social media were used in fundraising?

2. How important are MySpace, Twitter, Facebook, YouTube, blogging, and other social media in other countries?

3. Ask older communications professionals—journalists, PR practitioners—about communications tools of 10, 20, 30, 40 years ago. Track progress.

4. Study blogs of various issues and various companies. Do criticized companies and persons respond effectively? This may be because blogging is relatively new, and many have not caught up with the technique or the necessity. Discuss with others in class.

5. Study websites. Do they paint a positive picture of the organization? Do they address issues and problems, or are they puffery? Are they easy to maneuver around? Are they more glitz than substance? Are they easy to read, with lists, bulleted points, and brief sentences? What are the negative and positive points of the site? Do sites have crisis prevention data, or information about current or past crises?

Discussion and Essays

1. Considering the Rescola story, what should offices in skyscrapers and large buildings do other than plan for evacuation? Imagine the employees who objected to the training: what would be persuasive messages to them? The 1993 attack was considered a prodrome by Rescola. Why didn't others see it?

2. Pick well-known crises in history and discuss how social media could have been used if such media had existed; for example, the Titanic striking the iceberg.

3. Similar but opposite to #3 under Activities, imagine what will be the primary means of crisis communications in 10 years, 20 years. What will be the status of newspapers, TV news, social media? Which, if any, of the current social media will survive? Will news media eventually become citizen media only? What are the problems of citizen journalists now? Will those problems be compounded in the future, or will there be solutions?

4. When the textbook went to press, there were no actual rules of social media. Have any been developed? What rules should be developed?

5. Have students used social media in their personal crises? Which social media? To what effect?

Vocabulary

golden hour _____

_____

_____

_____

_____

Internet protocol _____

_____

_____

_____

_____

crisis _____

_____

_____

_____

_____

crisis communications _____

_____

_____

_____

_____

crisis management _____

_____

_____

_____

_____

Crisis Communications Plan _____

_____

_____

_____

_____

_____

public relations _____

_____

_____

_____

_____

_____

media relations _____

_____

_____

_____

_____

_____

community relations _____

_____

_____

_____

_____

_____

employee relations _____

_____

_____

_____

_____

_____

internal relations _____

_____

_____

_____

_____

_____

consumer relations _____

_____

_____

_____

_____

_____

publics _____

_____

_____

_____

_____

_____

prodrome _____

_____

_____

_____

_____

_____

prodromal stage of a crisis _____

_____

_____

_____

_____

_____

detection stage of a crisis _____

_____

_____

_____

_____

_____

prevention/preparation stage of a crisis _____

_____

_____

_____

_____

_____

containment stage of a crisis _____

_____

_____

_____

_____

_____

recovery stage of a crisis _____

_____

_____

_____

_____

_____

learning stage of a crisis _____

_____

_____

_____

_____

_____

public opinion _____

_____

_____

_____

_____

_____

Chapter 2

Crisis Communications Theory

A spokesperson for a ski resort, The Summit at Snoqualmie, near Seattle, issued a statement to the news media after a 29-year-old man died on its slopes in late 2005. The statement said the man was on his own when he ventured into a closed area where he was later found. This led the news media to conclude that he had broken the rules. Later, the resort learned that he was part of a team, having been invited by two experienced ski patrollers.

Later, the resort, though not responsible for the death, purchased an ad in the *Seattle Times* (6/19/06) with the headline, "The Summit at Snoqualmie acknowledges that David W. Pettigrew's tragic snowboarding accident did not result from David breaking any rules."

The first of 12 paragraphs read, "On December 7, 2005, 29-year-old David W. Pettigrew died in a tragic accident at Alpental Ski Area at the Summit at Snoqualmie. Directly following his death, statements to the press by the ski resort said David was on his own when he ventured into a closed area where he was later found. These initial statements by the ski resort were not accurate and were incomplete. They led the news media to the mistaken conclusion that David was responsible for his own death by skiing alone in a roped-off area."

Following was a quote, an apology from the general manager, who said, "We later learned the details, but unfortunately, we weren't pro-active. We didn't go back and try to get the details out that would clear David's reputation." And ". . . We are very sorry, and we want to set the record straight . . ."

The half-page story then described how the tragedy occurred in some detail and how David's family and friends felt the news coverage tarnished his memory, and ended with about five paragraphs describing what a wonderful person David was. A photo of David was at the top of the ad.

Activities

1. Consider recent crises or crises in the textbook and draft explanations that would not be full and contrite apologies but that would be categorized as apologia theory responses.

2. How have social media impacted the excellence theory? Find examples of Model 4 practice online that did not exist prior to the development of social media. Which of the social media lends itself best to the excellence theory? And to the apologia theory?

3. Can you find any evidence of professional use of Model 1 of the excellence theory?

4. Read the theatre scenario in the *diffusion theory* section and conceive a *diffusion of innovation theory* for some problem at your university, community, or city.

5. Examine organizations in the textbook that suffered news-making crises and note their compliance or noncompliance with characteristics espoused by crisis communications theorists. The following are characteristics of the excellence theory; however, characteristics can also be developed for the other theories. The study is intended to aid the understanding and discussion of crisis communications theories as they apply to each case.

   a Was the head of communications important to top management?

   b Did the communications department, prior to the crisis, identify its key stakeholders and rank them in order of importance?

   c Were there, prior to the crisis, communications programs designed to build relationships with all key stakeholders?

   d Were there strong relationships with stakeholders?

   e Were there strong relationships with the news media?

   f Were publics segmented into more manageable and reachable bodies for ongoing communications programs?

   g Did the organization have a Crisis Communications Plan in place prior to the crisis?

   h Was issues management practiced prior to the crisis?

   i Were two-way communication ideologies established prior to the crisis? Segment the student body of your college or university into bodies that can be reached more effectively and more directly and personally than the news media.

Discussion and Essays

1. Does "I'm sorry," used in tweets and other social media, seem insincere? Are tweets too brief to be fully expressive?

2. In apologia theory, how can an organization respond apologetically without admitting guilt? Create scenarios and discuss.

3. What are some examples of redefinition you can recall organizations using?

4. What are some examples of dissociation you can recall organizations using?

5. What are some examples of conciliation you can recall organizations using?

6. In a crisis situation, using the image restoration theory, how could an organization determine which publics should receive which messages? Why would you send different messages to different publics?

7. For what types of crisis would the diffusion theory be most appropriate? Least appropriate?

8. What makes it difficult to use Model 4 of the excellence theory in a crisis?

9. What model of the excellence theory is likely the most popular model used during times of crisis?

10. Why do many professionals not use theory?

Vocabulary

theory _____

_____

_____

_____

_____

_____

apologia theory _____

_____

_____

_____

_____

redefinition _____

_____

_____

_____

_____

_____

dissociation _____

_____

_____

_____

_____

_____

conciliation _____

_____

_____

_____

_____

_____

image restoration theory _____

_____

_____

_____

_____

_____

decision theory _____

_____

_____

_____

_____

_____

RACE _____

_____

_____

_____

_____

_____

ROPE _____

_____

_____

_____

_____

_____

maximizing _____

_____

_____

_____

_____

_____

satisficing _____

_____

_____

_____

_____

_____

diffusion theory _____

_____

_____

_____

_____

_____

change agents _____

_____

_____

_____

_____

_____

excellence theory _____

_____

_____

_____

_____

_____

strategy _____

_____

_____

_____

_____

_____

stakeholders _____

_____

_____

_____

_____

_____

strategic publics _____

_____

_____

_____

_____

_____

strategically managed public relations _____

_____

_____

_____

_____

_____

segmentation _____

_____

_____

_____

_____

_____

risk communications _____

_____

_____

_____

_____

_____

organizational ideology _____

_____

_____

_____

_____

_____

communications ideology _____

_____

_____

_____

_____

_____

Chapter 3

Communications to Prevent Crises

Activity

1. Look at various corporate and organizational websites and notice how important employees are to the organization. Are there indicators that employees are a key concern? Or are the employees merely a means to helping the company succeed? What are some methods of building relationships with employees? What communications can help with that relationship-building? Would it matter to external publics what the relationship is between a company and its employees? Why or why not?

Discussion and Essays

1. In these days of swift delivery of information, often the news media inform the organization of its crisis. What are the advantages of knowing about your crisis before the news media? This also points to the need to have a positive relationship with the news media, so that you may be notified before or as soon as news is delivered via broadcast or Internet (see Johnson & Johnson and the Tylenol Murders, Chapter 7). What should an organization do to maintain this positive relationship?

2. Evaluate the pre-crisis relationships at the places of business where you have worked (or where you work now). Were the pre-crisis relationships sound? Consider all types, including management–employee, management–news media, management–lawyer, and management–customer/client pre-crisis relationships.

3. When you speak about your company, do you say, "We do this" or "They do this"? What does your response to this question say about how involved you are with your company, or how important you feel you are to your company?

Vocabulary

pro-active public relations _____

_____

_____

_____

_____

people-centered corporate culture _____

_____

_____

_____

_____

Chapter 4

Communications When the Crisis Strikes

Activities

1. Create a crisis scenario at a local company or business. Who would be the possible spokespersons? Use titles or positions; names are not important. Look at the Snapps crisis (see textbook page 66).

2. Often, the public is unaware of conflicts between spokespersons and lawyers in news-making crises. Examine recent crises and imagine what conflicts there could have been.

3. Select a restaurant in your community. Suppose that restaurant suffered a fire that was widely reported. Other than ads (which may or may not be affordable), how could the restaurant management let customers know they are open for business? Should restaurants keep a list of regular patrons? How would they get such a list? As a project, help a small restaurant develop a patron list.

Discussion and Essays

1. What are the risks or dangers of not responding to the news media, even when the information is negative to your organization? Why is it best to tell one's own bad news?

2. Why will a people-centered company or organization be advantageous in a crisis?

3. What are possible occasions when the CEO is not the best spokesperson after a crisis?

Vocabulary

apology versus excuse _____

_____

_____

_____

_____

prodromes _____

_____

_____

_____

_____

people-centered culture _____

_____

_____

_____

_____

profit-centered culture _____

_____

_____

_____

_____

spokespersons _____

_____

_____

_____

_____

key messages _____

_____

_____

_____

_____

speaking points _____

_____

_____

_____

_____

trick questions (rude q's) _____

_____

_____

_____

_____

speculative questions _____

_____

_____

_____

_____

leading questions _____

_____

_____

_____

_____

naïve questions _____

_____

_____

_____

_____

false questions _____

_____

_____

_____

_____

know-it-all questions _____

_____

_____

_____

_____

silence after a question _____

_____

_____

_____

_____

accusatory questions _____

_____

_____

_____

_____

multiple-part questions _____

_____

_____

_____

_____

jargonistic questions _____

_____

_____

_____

_____

chummy questions _____

_____

_____

_____

_____

labeling questions _____

_____

_____

_____

_____

good-bye questions _____

_____

_____

_____

_____

APR designation _____

_____

_____

_____

_____

Public Relations Society of America _____

_____

_____

_____

_____

consumer policy _____

_____

_____

_____

_____

consumer relations _____

_____

_____

_____

_____

blogs _____

_____

_____

_____

_____

corporate/organizational blog _____

_____

_____

_____

_____

subject blog _____

_____

_____

_____

_____

industry blog _____

_____

_____

_____

_____

publication blog _____

_____

_____

_____

_____

personal blog _____

_____

_____

_____

_____

Chapter 5

Social Media and Crisis Communications

Activities

1. Find out how local organizations use social media in a crisis. Ask communicators (PR professionals, executives, legal representatives).

2. Research news-making crises and how social media helped. Which social media were used?

3. Look up websites of companies mentioned in the chapter and see if there are still any lingering posts, blogs, etc., on the crises covered. Were additional actions taken by the company? Did additional problems or crises develop? Was the problem mentioned in the chapter a prodrome (warning sign) for another crisis or problem?

4. Write tweets relating to the crises in the chapter to solve, apologize, mend damage. Be sure to adhere to the character limit.

5. Look up ways social media were used after disasters: Haitian earthquake of 2010, Chilean earthquake and tsunami of 2010, more recent disasters.

Discussion and Essays

1. Discuss crises for which social media would not be the best methods of communication.

2. Would a crisis communications plan have helped any of the companies mentioned in this chapter? Why, or why not?

3. Did the companies in the chapter reach a larger public through social media? A more crucial public? What are the characteristics of the public reached?

4. Discuss related issues, such as cases of MySpace bullying.

5. Is there a difference in how people will accept bad news via social media rather than traditional media? Can you assume most people will be alerted first by traditional media, then seek additional explanation through social media?

6. Government agencies, such as the Centers for Disease Control (CDC), and many companies must have communications approved by various levels of authorities before release by social or traditional media. This takes time. Should they decrease or eliminate this approval process, release the best information possible, no matter how vague or erroneous it might be, and expand or correct later? What are the pros and cons of early release versus later release?

Southwest Airlines Case

7. If the comments had been negative, how should the communicators at Southwest Airlines have reacted?

8. Should Southwest Airlines communicate with the pilots and flight attendants? What would be the purpose and the key messages?

Coca-Cola Case

9. The customer had 10,000 Twitter followers. Is that a magic number? How many Twitter followers must a customer have to make a company act?

Jet Blue Case

10. Suppose all or most passengers on an airline took the action of Tony Wagner? Would Jet Blue still be pleased? What would happen? What should happen?

11. Suppose changing seats was not possible. What could be Jet Blue's communications?

University of California, San Diego

12. How should the University of California communicate with students who were told they were admitted when they were not?

Chapter 6

Rumors and Cybercrises

Activities

1. Find a rogue website on the Internet and describe your response to it. Write a response that could be printed in a newspaper, circulated via e-mail, or posted on a website. Which method of responding would be most effective and why?

2. Search the Internet for other rogue websites. Consider why the sites were created and by whom (e.g., angry ex-employees, disgruntled customers). Also search the Internet for evidence that the organizations or companies attacked defended themselves (e.g., check their websites for responses to the attack sites). What damage could be done to the organizations attacked? If you were hired by one of these companies or organizations to remedy the situation, what would you do?

3. Research damaging rumors you have heard about companies, organizations, and individuals and try to determine their origin. If the rumors are false, how could they have been stopped or alleviated? Did you believe the rumor initially? Why or why not?

4. Check the CDC website for issues similar to the e-mail hoax discussed in Mini-Case: The Killer Banana Rumor (Figure 6.2). Discuss how that hoax could have affected the banana industry. How can such hoaxes affect the economy?

5. The following are some comments by experts on the killer banana e-mail hoax. Which comments are convincing to a person who might believe the hoax and which comments are unconvincing? These quotes were reported on APBNews.com (Noack, 2000).

   a Tim Debus, vice president of the International Banana Association (IBA): "The rumor is just another case of Internet terrorism like the recent hacker attacks on popular Web sites."

   b CDC and the Food and Drug Administration (FDA) advisory board: "FDA and CDC agree that the bacteria [necrotizing fasciitis] cannot survive long on the surface of a banana. The usual route of transmission for these bacteria is from person to person."

c   John Shieh, a consultant to the Foundation: "The mere ingestion of these bacteria would only make you sick with vomiting and diarrhea. [Eating] will not cause you to get a necrotizing fasciitis. Don't worry about the bananas, anyway. Most of them you buy are from the USA."

d   Chiquita Brands International (CBI): "The report currently circulating on the Internet concerning Costa Rican bananas being contaminated with a rare bacteria is totally false. Chiquita has received no reports of such contamination, and we have checked with the pertinent U.S. government agencies, which also confirm no reports of such contamination."

6.   Read the e-mail rumor shown in Figure 6.3. Make a list of all the outrageous claims mentioned in the message.

7.   Read the U.S. Postal Service news release shown in Figure 6.4. This rumor has been repeated via e-mail for many years. See if you can find anything on the USP website about other rumors. What makes people believe this rumor and pass it on?

Discussion and Essays

1.   What laws protect companies and organizations from rogue websites and e-mail rumors? What laws protect consumers? What laws are needed to ensure protection?

2.   What damaging rumors have you heard about companies, organizations, or individuals that could cause problems similar to those suffered by Snapps? Did you believe the rumors? What could be done to prove or disprove the rumors? Is there a move to do that?

3.   Was it wise for Snapps to hold a news conference? What else might it have done to alleviate the crisis?

4.   What type of person could have started the rumor and why?

5.   What elements of the message in Figure 6.1 seem designed to make you believe the bank is helping you out of a problem? Why are no phone numbers and no names given? How would you explain that the URL in the message seems real?

Phishing

This is the actual wording from a phishing scam sent via e-mail. We are using the name of a fictional bank, Phonybank. Read the e-mail (shown on p. 28) and then respond to the questions listed.

Please note: Documents such as Figure 6.1–6.4 usually have typos, misspellings, and grammatical errors. How many such errors can you find?

Date: Wed, 26 January 2010 15:59:47–0500

From: Phonybank clientdepartment@Phonybank.com

Dear Phonybank customer,

We recently noticed one or more attempts to log in to your Phonybank account from a foreign IP address and we have reasons to believe that your account was hijacked by a third party without your authorization.

If you recently accessed your account while traveling, the unusual log-in attempts may have been initiated by you. However, if you are the rightful holder of the account, click on the link below and submit, as we try to verify your account.

https://accounts4.Phonybank.com/uuu/controller?request

The log in attempt was made from:

IP address: 55.555.55.555

ISP host: 66.666.66.666fool. net

If you choose to ignore our request, you leave us no choice but to temporary suspend your account.

We ask that you allow at least 48 hours for the case to be investigated and we strongly recommend not making any changes to your account in that time.

If you received this notice and you are not the authorized account holder, please be aware that it is in violation of Phonybank policy to represent oneself as another Phonybank account holder. Such action may also be in violation of local, national, and/or international law. Phonybank is committed to assist law enforcement with any inquiries related to attempts to misappropriate personal information with the internet to commit fraud or theft.

Information will be provided at the request of law enforcement agencies to ensure that perpetrators are prosecuted to the fullest extent of the law.

Please do not respond to this email as your reply will not be received.

For assistance, log in to your Phonybank account and choose the "Help" link.

Thanks for your patience as we work together to protect your account.

Regards,

The Phonybank Team

Figure 6.1 Phishing Scam E-mail

Date: Thu, 24 Feb 2000 11:44:37 0500

From: XXXXX < XXXX@cdc.gov >

To: K. Fearn-Banks

Subject: FW: "Banana Warning"

Kathleen,

This is a false report. Please go to the CDC homepage, In the News, press releases. There is one dated Jan. 28 that addresses this.

http://www/cdc.gov/od/oc/meida/pressrel/r2ko 12 8.htm

In a message dated 2/14/00 6:58:14 PM Pacific Standard Time, XXX writes:

Vital Information regarding contaminated bananas. Please forward to everyone you love! I have checked the source and it is VALIDATED FROM THE CDC (Center for Disease Control in Atlanta, Georgia.)

Warning: Several shipments of bananas from Costa Rica have been infected with necrotizing fasciitis, otherwise known as flesh-eating bacteria. Recently this disease has decimated the monkey population in Costa Rica. We are now just learning that the disease has been able to graft itself to the skin of fruits in the region, most notably the banana, which is Costa Rica's largest export. Until this finding, scientists were not sure how the infection was transmitted.

It is advised not to purchase bananas for the next three weeks as this is the period of time for which bananas that have been shipped to the United States with the possibility of carrying this disease. If you have eaten bananas in the last 2–3 days and come down with a fever followed by a skin infection, seek "Medical Attention."!!!

The skin infection from necrotizing fascitis is very painful and eats two to three centimeters of flesh per hour. Amputation is likely; death is possible. If you are more than an hour from a medical center, burning the flesh ahead of the infected area is advised to help slow the spread of the infection.

The FDA has been reluctant to issue to country-wide warning because of fear of nationwide panic. They have secretly admitted that they feel upwards of 15,000 American will be affected by this but that these are not acceptable numbers.

Figure 6.2 The Killer Banana e-mail hoax: this is a copy of the e-mail attack message on the banana industry circulated in early 2000. Names of persons were eliminated. Note that the Centers for Disease Control, which the letter said validated the "killer bananas," said the report is false. Like most e-mail hoaxes, this one cited a reliable source, the CDC. The message also contains several clues that the story was fabricated. What clues can you find in the letter?

Date:

From: XXXX

To: Kathleen Fearn-Banks

Subject: Info

You won't believe what happened to me yesterday. I was on my way to the post office to pick up my case of free M&M's (sent to me because I forwarded an e-mail to five other people, celebrating the fact that the year 2000 is "MM" in Roman numerals), when I ran into a friend whose neighbor, a young man, was home recovering from having been served a rat in his bucket of Kentucky Fried Chicken (which is predictable, since as everyone knows, there's no actual chicken in Kentucky Fried Chicken, which is why the government made them change their name to KFC).

Anyway, one day this guy went to sleep and when he awoke he was in his bathtub and it was full of ice and he was sore all over and when he got out of the tub he realized that HIS KIDNEY HAD BEEN STOLEN. He saw a note on his mirror that said "Call 911!" but he was afraid to use his phone because it was connected to his computer, and there was a virus on his computer that would destroy his hard drive if he opened an e-mail entitled "Join the crew!" He knew it wasn't a hoax because he himself was a computer programmer who was working on software to prevent a global disaster in which all the computers get together and distribute the $250.00 Neiman–Marcus cookie recipe under the leadership of Bill Gates. (It's true—I read it all last week in a mass e-mail from BILL GATES HIMSELF, who was also promising me a free Disney World vacation and $5,000 if I would forward the e-mail to everyone I know.)

The poor man then tried to call 911 from a pay phone to report his missing kidney, but a voice on the line first asked him to press #90, which unwittingly gave the bandit full access to the phone line at the guy's expense. Then reaching into the coin return slot he got jabbed with an HIV-infected needle around which was wrapped a note that said, "Welcome to the world of AIDS."

Luckily he was only a few blocks from the hospital—the one where that little boy who is dying of cancer is, the one whose last wish is for everyone in the world to send him an e-mail and the American Cancer Society has agreed to pay him a nickel for every e-mail he receives. I sent him two e-mails and one of them was a bunch of X's and O's in the shape of an angel (if you get it forward it to more than 10 people you will have good luck, but for 10 people only you will have OK luck, and if you send it to fewer than 10 people you will have BAD LUCK FOR SEVEN YEARS). So anyway the poor guy tried to drive himself to the hospital, but on the way he noticed another car driving without its lights on. To be helpful, he flashed his lights at him and was promptly shot as part of a gang initiation.

Send THIS to all the friends who send you their junk mail and you will receive 4 green M&M's. If you don't the owner of Proctor and Gamble will report you to his Satanist friends and you will have more bad luck: you will get sick from the Sodium Laureth Sulfate in your shampoo, your spouse/mate will develop a skin rash from using the antiperspirant which clogs the pores under your arms, and the U.S. government will put a tax on your e-mails forever.

I know this is all true 'cause I read it on the Internet and in e-mail.

Figure 6.3 This e-mail letter, obviously intended as a joke, was circulated widely and taken seriously by numerous people, who passed it on to friends hoping to warn them.

UNITED STATES

POSTAL SERVICE

Postal News

FOR IMMEDIATE RELEASE

May 21, 1999

Release No. 99–045

E-MAIL RUMOR COMPLETELY UNTRUE

WASHINGTON—A completely false rumor concerning the U.S. Postal Service is being circulated on Internet e-mail. As a matter of fact, the Postal Service has learned that a similar hoax occurred recently in Canada concerning Canada Post.

The e-mail message claims that a "Congressman Schnell" has introduced "Bill 602P" to allow the federal government to impose a 5-cent surcharge on each e-mail message delivered over the Internet. The money would be collected by Internet Service Providers and then turned over to the Postal Service.

No such proposed legislation exists. In fact, no "Congressman Schnell" exists.

The U.S. Postal Service has no authority to surcharge e-mail messages sent over the Internet, nor would it support such legislation.

# # #

Figure 6.4 The U.S. Postal Service disseminated this news release on May 21, 1999, in an attempt to stop an unfounded e-mail rumor.

(Source: U.S. Postal Service Web page **www.usps.com/news/email.htm**. Reprinted by permission.)

Vocabulary

Anticybersquatting Consumer Protection Act of 1999 _____

_____

_____

_____

_____

domain names _____

_____

_____

_____

_____

phishing _____

_____

_____

_____

_____

rogue website _____

_____

_____

_____

_____

search engine _____

_____

_____

_____

_____

spoof sites _____

_____

_____

_____

_____

suck sites _____

_____

_____

_____

_____

war of public opinion _____

_____

_____

_____

_____

Chapter 7

"Textbook" Crises

Case: Johnson & Johnson and the Tylenol Murders

This early case of crisis communications shows how one company with a strong communication ideology used communications to recover from a crisis, despite the fact that it had no crisis plan. It reveals how ethical behavior, or "doing the right thing," pays off.

Activities

1. For groups: After the tampering crisis, you are hired by Johnson & Johnson to help relaunch Tylenol in a new safety-sealed container. Research reveals that the consumer public must be "sold" on the product's safety. What would you do to "sell" the public on Tylenol?

2. Check the Johnson & Johnson website at **www.johnsonandjohnson.com** and **www.tylenol.com**. Is there any reference to the Tylenol-tampering case, which was never solved, or the $100,000 reward? Are there more recent issues that could be prodromes to other crises? Do you see the same "open and honest" policy with the news media and consumer publics that existed during the crisis?

3. Check the websites of other pharmaceutical companies for information about product tampering and product failure, communication ideology, and so on. Compare and contrast what you find at the various pharmaceutical websites, including the Johnson & Johnson site.

4. After the Tylenol-tampering crisis, Johnson & Johnson officials said that a crisis communications plan would not have helped with their particular crisis. Do you agree? Why or why not?

5. There were numerous copycat tamperings following the Tylenol crisis. Has there been a product tampering in your city or state? What was the outcome? Was the company honest and open with the news media?

6. Look for articles about product tamperings on the Internet. Discuss the media's coverage.

7. In 1997, Johnson & Johnson informed consumers— through advertisements, product labels, public service announcements (PSAs)—that too much Tylenol can be harmful to children. Using the following list of facts, write a Twitter message for customers. (You may not need to use all the information given here.)

a A new infant Tylenol formula is expected to reach stores in 6–7 weeks.

b Taking more than the recommended dosage can cause serious health risks.

c Acetaminophen, Tylenol's active ingredient, has been blamed for liver damage and even deaths in children. The ingredient is also in Anacin 3 and other pain relievers.

d The FDA admits that accurate dosages are very effective.

e The FDA advised manufacturers of acetaminophen to make changes in product labeling to warn parents. Johnson & Johnson's new product labels do just that.

Discussion and Essays

I. Discuss how the Tylenol case applies to the crisis communications theories covered in Chapter 2.

2. If the Tylenol crisis occurred today, would you expect the news media to be as cooperative as they were in 1982? Why or why not?

Vocabulary

credo _____

_____

_____

_____

_____

product recall _____

_____

_____

_____

_____

Case: *Exxon* and the *Valdez* Oil Spill

Activities

1. An Associated Press story, "Oil spill largest ever on Alaska's North Slope," ran in the *Seattle Times* on page B2 on Saturday, March 11, 2006. Here are the first four paragraphs:

> Anchorage—An oil spill discovered this month in Alaska's Prudloe Bay is the largest ever on the North Slope, according to an official estimate released Friday.
>
> The estimated spill size of 201,000 to 267,000 gallons far surpasses the 38,000 spilled in 2001, but it is much less than the 11 million gallons spilled in Prince William Sound when the *Exxon Valdez* ran aground in 1989.
>
> The North Slope is the region between the Brooks Range and the Arctic Ocean and contains most of Alaska's petroleum reserves.
>
> "I can confirm it's the largest spill of crude oil on the North Slope that we have record of," said Linda Giguere of the state Department of Environmental Conservation. The state has kept comprehensive records of oil spills for a decade, with more cursory record-keeping dating to the 1970s, when the trans-Alaska oil pipeline was built.

Discussion and Essays

1. What is not mentioned? How does this compare with the *Exxon Valdez* oil spill and why? What about the page number of the article?

Chapter 8

Culture Crises
Foreign and Domestic

Case: Saginaw Valley State University and the Theater Controversy

Activities

1. Analyze the open letter written by the university's president (see Figure 8.1, p. 38).

2. Notice the first paragraph and the final paragraph are polite, gracious expressions. The letter was written primarily for people who object to the play; they are an angry public. So, why does he open and close the letter with these expressions?

3. Paragraphs 2 through 6 explain why the play was chosen and why it will still run, despite objections. Paragraph 2 mentions what the Theater Department has done in the past. Out of all the productions the department has done over many years, why does he mention these plays and performances at the children's zoo?

4. In paragraphs 3 and 4, how do the following words and phrases contribute to the overall effect of the letter: wonderful range, comprehensive, art, controversial, unnerving, occasionally even raw, sheltered and incomplete, raise troublesome questions?

5. Paragraph 5 of the open letter from the president admits a mistake on the part of the director in doing the interview below. What was this?

6. Figure 8.2 shows the first part of the interview with Richard Roberts, director of *Angels in America Part One: Millennium Approaches*, by Janet Martineau, in the *Saginaw News* on Saturday, April 14, 2007. Some words are paraphrased and in brackets.

7. Paragraph 6 expresses the president's ire. He lets readers know he has had it. You can visualize his anger over having to write such a letter and you certainly see why he didn't respond personally to objectors. Was he too angry, not angry enough, or is the letter just about right?

AN OPEN LETTER

I appreciate your thoughtful expression of concern. It is a freedom of expression issue, but some additional context may also be helpful in your assessment of our theater program at SVSU.

Our Theater Department has attempted to give our students a balanced and varied array of performance opportunities. In the past few years, they have performed children's productions ("Princess and the Pea," "Young Black Beauty"), musicals ("Oliver," "Man of La Mancha," "Fiddler on the Roof"), comedies ("I Ought to be in Pictures," "I Love You, You're Perfect, Now Change"), seasonal works ("A Christmas Carol"), and even informal performances for kids at the Saginaw Children's Zoo.

All in all, our students have had a wonderful range of opportunities to experience the varieties of theater. But part of any comprehensive range of performance art must also include pieces that may be more controversial, unnerving, occasionally even raw. Their experiences would be sheltered and incomplete without exposure to contemporary plays that raise troublesome questions—even in controversial ways.

"Angels in America" is such a play, but it was carefully chosen. It also won a Pulitzer Prize and several other awards, and has served as the basis for a television mini-series.

In the local news report about this production, the Director tried to give the readers fair warning as to what was in the play so that all of us could make an informal judgment about whether we wanted to attend. I appreciate his doing that. Certainly no one should be lured into a performance only to be offended.

And so, I suspect we may simply have to remain in disagreement about this matter. But even as I am not willing to censor this kind of artistic expression, you too are free to express your disapproval. And I do respect your point of view in this regard.

Again, thank you for your message and your thoughtfulness in expressing it.

Sincerely,

Eric Gilbertson
PRESIDENT
Saginaw Valley State University

Figure 8.1 Open letter from the university president to alleviate the crisis.

A play "clearly no community theater north of Detroit would touch" opens a two-weekend run Friday at Saginaw Valley State University.

And, says [director Roberts] not only is it untouchable at community theaters—it's also R-rated territory and suitable only for ages 16 and up.

Tony Kushner's [play] is a challenge on all fronts.

It runs three hours. It's subtitled as a "gay fantasia" and, as such, deals with homosexuality and the HIV/AIDS crisis in its early days. It needles Republicans, features ghosts and angels, and travels to several locations throughout the world, Antarctica among them.

It also includes full-frontal male nudity and the use of the F word in every way possible—without either being gratuitous, says Roberts.

"And we are doing it all," says Roberts. "It is our responsibility to provide our students with cutting edge material to perform, with shows that stretch them.

"We are the only theater in mid-Michigan that can get away with it because, while we want people to come see the show, we're not tied to ticket sales to survive. I relish doing this."

The rest of the story primarily discussed the actors.

Figure 8.2 Interview with the director of the play. Published in the Saginaw News.

Discussion and Essays

1. Some colleges would not be able to produce *Angels in America*. Has your college or university ever presented this or other controversial plays? If so, were they well received by the student body, by the community, by the news media?

2. How does acceptance of a play like this vary at a public university or a private one? What about a religious college or university?

3. How does the culture of the surrounding community affect this acceptance?

4. What about the educational level of community members? Does that matter?

5. Does it matter that people in the community have lived in the same community all their lives, have never lived elsewhere, rarely traveled?

6. Does it matter if there is a significant gay/lesbian presence in the community and how it is accepted?

7. Would it matter to theater patrons that the key actors were not both gay?

Case: AIDS in Africa

This case study looks at cultural characteristics of persons living in various African countries, how these characteristics affect the fight against HIV/AIDS, and how communications programs have to be structured to bring about progress. The thread running through the study is that, whether foreign or domestic, communicators must research their publics thoroughly before beginning a crisis communications campaign.

Box 8.1 Twenty-Five Years of the HIV/AIDS Pandemic

The AIDS pandemic reached its twenty-fifth anniversary in 2006, as the United Nations conference on AIDS met in New York in May. According to the UNAIDS report, globally, 65 million people had been infected, and 25 million had died. Infection rates were falling in some African countries owing to modified behavior among African youths. This points to the success of some of the communications programs in this chapter.

Uganda and Zimbabwe were among the most successful countries with prevention programs. HIV prevalence—the proportion of the population infected—dropped by more than a quarter in these countries among people aged 15–24. The decline was attributed to increased condom use, less casual sex, and a delay in the beginning of sexual activity. Both men and women have reduced their numbers of sexual partners, but Adrienne Germain, of the International Women's Health Coalition, observed that Uganda would not have made such progress without condoms in the curriculum.

Not all countries have found success in the programs. Howard LaFranchi, in the *Christian Science Monitor* (5/31/06) wrote, ". . . many development and health groups focused on Africa are critical of U.S. policy. They say it favors a wasteful, unilateral approach instead of joining existing AIDS programs. Beyond that, they argue that U.S. policy harbors an ideological 'abstinence only' bent in prevention work that undermines the widely favored ABC approach . . ."

In the United States, AIDS is the leading cause of death among African–American women aged 25–34, noted Yolanda Richardson at the Centre for Development and Population Activities. Richardson said these infection rates are climbing: "we can say that our conventional strategies are not working because they are not working for women." Half of all people with the virus are women, as compared with 41 percent in 1997 and 35 percent in 1985. Austin Ruse at the Catholic Family and Human Rights Institute said that the push for condoms is not working. "The world is flooded with condoms, but it doesn't seem to have much impact on the HIV rate."

Box 8.1—*continued*

India has become the country with the greatest number of HIV cases: 5.7 million, as compared with 5.5 million in sub-Saharan Africa. However, the African countries, with a total population of 45 million people, have more HIV cases per capita than India with a population of 1 billion. A third of adults in Southern Africa are infected, compared with less than 1 percent in India.

The communications efforts in 4 of India's 28 states have resulted in a decline from 1.7 percent to 1.1 percent between 2000 and 2004. The publics successfully targeted in Andhra Pradesh, Karnataka, Maharashtra, and Tamil Nadu were prostitutes and the men who frequent them. Free condoms were distributed by the government. Non-governmental groups educate sex workers with posters and street-theater performances. The rest of the country shows an increase in new infections, indicating that the prevention communications programs worked in areas where they were used. Treatment has failed particularly among pregnant women, who can block mother-to-child transmission with a relatively inexpensive drug regimen. Only 9 percent of women are receiving the drug.

(The information was taken from articles by Thomas H. Maugh in the *Los Angeles Times* and Howard LaFranchi in the *Christian Science Monitor,* on May 31, 2006.)

Discussion and Essays

1. Look up and discuss the latest statistics on AIDS and HIV in African countries. Some statistics have improved; others have not.

2. What information in the above data shows a "disconnect"?

3. Why do you think more progress has been made in Uganda and Zimbabwe than in programs in the other countries studied?

4. What communications tactics could be adopted to address pregnant women in India?

5. From the textbook information, examine tactics used in one country that would not be effective in another country owing to differences in lifestyles.

6. Can you think of communications tactics that might be effective in a specific African country and were not mentioned in the chapter? How would you suggest these tactics be introduced to the country's citizens? Would the tactics address a broad public or a segmented public?

7. How do you explain the differences of opinion of Austin Ruse and Adrienne Germain?

Box 8.2 Children and AIDS

"Children are the missing face of the AIDS pandemic," said Ann Veneman, executive director of UNICEF.

A report issued on May 26, 2006, from the Global Movement for Children, revealed that more than 2 million children under the age of 15 were living with AIDS; most were in sub-Saharan Africa and have no access to treatment, making death certain.

The movement, made up of seven organizations, urged governments, donors, and the pharmaceutical industry to heed the crisis. There are antiretroviral treatments and antibiotics that can save or prolong life, but fewer than 5 percent of HIV-positive children have access to them. Most of these children will die before their fifth birthday.

World leaders of the seven richest industrialized nations and Russia pledged to seek universal treatment by 2010. African governments also pledged to spend 15 percent of their budgets on public health systems, but, according to the report, less than one-third have complied.

Discussion

Most reports, including the textbook chapter, imply that the greatest problems facing Africa's children are losing parents and security. Little has been said about HIV infection among children.

1. Who would be the publics targeted?

2. What tactics would likely be effective? Ineffective?

Instructors: To answer the above questions, it would be more effective to select specific countries, considering given cultural limitations, when developing tactics.

Box 8.3 HIV Jumped From Chimps to Humans

In 2006, 25 years after the first AIDS cases emerged, scientists confirmed that HIV originated in wild chimpanzees in the African country Cameroon.

According to the journal *Science*, Dr. Beatrice Hahn, University of Alabama, Birmingham, studied non-human primates with SIV, simian immunodeficiency virus. "The genetic similarity is striking," she said.

Apparently, a human in rural Cameroon was bitten by a chimp, or was cut while butchering a chimp, and became infected with the ape virus. That person passed it to someone else. This explains the jump from animal to human. The virus was passed to persons along the Sanaga River, a commercial waterway, and eventually made its way to Kinshasa in the Congo and the first known human with HIV.

There are no available data on how many people were infected between the first in Cameroon and the first patient identified with the disease in the Congo. Patient 1's blood was stored in 1959 as part of a medical study, long before scientists knew HIV existed.

The virus became more deadly to people than chimps, who seldom are bothered much by SIV.

Anthony Fauci, AIDS chief at the National Institute of Health, said the research seems to settle any question of HIV's origin.

Discussion and Essays

1. Scientists say these data may help them find a cure; it's one step toward that progress. Does knowing the origin of the virus change anything in the eyes of the public?

2. Will this data help or hinder communication urging celibacy and safe sex?

3. What does it indicate about the possible spread of the bird flu?

4. What other methods and messages can you suggest for prevention and for getting tested and treated? Many African countries are experiencing widespread use of the cell phone. How can the cell phone be useful in communicating information?

HIV/AIDS Timeline

Activities

1.   Timelines are frequent communications tools during crises. (See timeline in textbook for Hurricane Katrina and New Orleans on pages 180–181.) Below is the beginning of an HIV/AIDS timeline. Develop a more complete timeline for Africa, or the United States, the world, or any specific country. Clues: A famous athlete announced he was HIV-positive and changed the public perception of the HIV victim; the Highly Active Antiretroviral Therapy (HAART) was approved; and the CDC announced its first decline in deaths due to HAART.

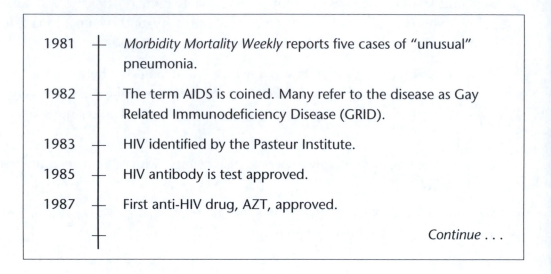

1981	*Morbidity Mortality Weekly* reports five cases of "unusual" pneumonia.
1982	The term AIDS is coined. Many refer to the disease as Gay Related Immunodeficiency Disease (GRID).
1983	HIV identified by the Pasteur Institute.
1985	HIV antibody is test approved.
1987	First anti-HIV drug, AZT, approved.
	Continue . . .

2.   Research communications tactics related to HIV/AIDS in other African countries and other continents.

Vocabulary

HIV _____

_____

_____

_____

_____

AIDS _____

_____

_____

_____

"disconnect" _____

_____

_____

_____

HIV prevalence _____

_____

_____

_____

do-gooders _____

_____

_____

_____

"slim disease" _____

_____

_____

_____

ABC strategy _____

_____

_____

_____

UNAIDS _____

_____

_____

_____

_____

virgin scholarship _____

_____

_____

_____

_____

Case: Texas A&M University and the Bonfire Tragedy

This case is a study of a long-held tradition, a rivalry of universities and their sports programs. It is a distinct culture among Texans. See Box 8.4, pp. 48–49.

Activities

1. Imagine that it is only a few days after the accident. Parents of deceased and injured students have been notified. Write a letter to the parents of students not injured in the bonfire tragedy. Although these parents already know their children were not harmed, they need some reassurances.

2. Check the Texas A&M website (**www.tamu.edu**) for information on the bonfire and other traditions. Prepare to discuss the pros and cons of these traditions in preparation for class discussion.

3. Read the news release "Texas A&M President's announcement about the decision on the future of bonfire" (Figure 8.4). Discuss. Which publics does the decision satisfy? In addition to safety precautions, what reasons might explain the university's decision to temporarily suspend the bonfire tradition?

4. Imagine that you are a spokesperson for Texas A&M University at the time of the crisis and that a news service from another state or country wants to run photos of students on your campus after it hears about the bonfire tragedy. Examine the four photos shown in Figure 8.3. Select the one photo that best says, "Our students are concerned about each other." Mark the photos that you do not want used because they say, "The university is a dangerous place." Would you allow the news service to use the photo of the female student with the cigarette in her hand? Why or why not?

Discussion and Essays

1. Cynthia Lawson, in a previous job, was part of a mock crisis. If she were to plan a mock crisis at Texas A&M, how could it work? Who would be the players? What information would it reveal? How could it help the university prevent or cope with future crises?

2. What traditions exist at your university? In your town or locality? What is the culture of your university and/or community? Would outsiders find it surprising? Look not only at activities but also at clothing styles, foods, hobbies, and the like. Students (like most other people) tend to see their lifestyles as normal and not worthy of discussion, whereas they see other cultures as different, strange, or difficult to understand.

3. The work of the Special Commission was reported on Texas A&M University Relations letterhead. Was this a good idea? Why or why not?

4. At a mock debriefing, discuss what Texas A&M University Relations might do in such a situation to avoid or deal with the conflict.

5. What area of campus life at your college or university could become a crisis? Are there prodromes? What would happen if a crisis were to occur? Which local reporters would be most likely to attack? If your university has a university relations officer, ask him or her to speak to the class about crises that have occurred and crises that were prevented.

Box 8.4 Texas A&M President Postpones Bonfire For 2 Years

COLLEGE STATION—Texas A&M University will suspend its traditional bonfire for two years, President Ray M. Bowen announced Friday during a news conference.

Bowen said the postponement of the bonfire until 2002 at the earliest was necessary because restructuring the design and planning construction of the event could not be properly done until that time.

"If the restructuring I have described is successfully completed, we will have a bonfire in 2002," Bowen said. "If that construction is judged successful by the certification process, then we will have a 2003 construction.

"You can expect important memorials and other events to occur in 2000 and 2001. The details of these events will need to be developed by our students," Bowen added.

On Nov. 18, 1999, the bonfire stack collapsed, killing 12 Aggies and injuring 27 others.

Bowen said significant changes will be required to ensure safe future bonfires. Among the changes he outlined were:

- A single tier "teepee" design.
- A bonfire construction plan prepared by licensed professionals.
- Construction time limited to two weeks, with no work performed after midnight.
- All logs will be cut by professionals and delivered to the construction site.
- The construction site will be a fenced-in area with limited access and monitored by video cameras.

Bowen said he will begin working with students, faculty, and staff to begin the planning of the 2002 bonfire, with their finalized plans due by April 2001.

He said his decision on the bonfire is not the defining event for the future of Texas A&M. "Our character as an academic institution of exceptional quality and our character as an academic institution that produces leaders are not dependent on the decision I announce today," he explained.

"The character of Texas A&M flows from the Aggie Spirit. This spirit is a manifestation of our academic strength, a manifestation of the character of the people of A&M, and [a] manifestation of our history and those uncountable intangibles that make Aggies special.

"My bonfire decision places great responsibility upon our student leadership," Bowen said.

This June 6, 2000 news release announced plans to suspend the Texas A&M bonfire tradition until at least 2002.

Box 8.4—*continued*

"It requires that they work with us to meet the conditions I have described. In doing so, they will be committing to fundamental changes in all aspects of the bonfire, changes which none of them would ever have anticipated before last Nov. 18. They will be required to commit to processes which protect not only the students [who] build the 2002 bonfire, but the students [who] will build all future bonfires.

"It will be their responsibility to implement the cultural change necessary to see that the horror of the bonfire collapse never visits our campus again."

Bowen said his decisions regarding the bonfire were not made in haste.

"I understand and respect the interest in this decision on the part of members of the A&M community," he said. "Our history and our traditions are important to all of us. The bonfire is one of the major traditions. It is not the defining activity of the university. It is one of many manifestations of what we call the 'Aggie Spirit.' If somehow we did not have a bonfire, the Aggie Spirit would manifest itself in another beneficial activity just as it does in so many others at Texas A&M. The special character of this university and its people is not, in my opinion, defined by any one tradition."

Bowen added, "I have heard from people who say this decision rivals the most difficult decisions that have been made throughout our history. People equate it with the decision to admit women and the decision to make the Corps of Cadets optional. I think that I am uniquely qualified to tell you that these assessments are wrong.

"**Frankly, the bold decisions which were made in the mid-to-late 1960s to commit Texas A&M to nationally prominent academic programs were more important to A&M than any decision on the bonfire.**"

Bowen said all of his decisions were based on "one simple truth: I do what is best for the university and its students. Regarding the advice I have received from the Aggie community, it is easy to summarize. A small number of people have advised me that the bonfire should be ended, a small number have said the bonfire should continue with minimum changes.

"The remainder, a vast number of people, have advised [me] to continue the bonfire only if it can be made a safe student activity. This large group advocates making whatever changes are necessary in order to have a safe bonfire."

He added, "It is my decision that this restructuring must produce a well-managed bonfire student project which is forever safe, which projects a positive image for the university and which does not place detrimental time demands on students."

Source: Texas A&M University Aggie Daily website: **www.tamu.edu/aggiedaily/press**. Reprinted by permission of Texas A&M Office of University Relations.

Figure 8.3 These four posed photos depict scenes of students reacting to word that several students on their campus were killed in a bonfire accident. (They are meant for discussion of photos only and in no way are intended as actual depictions of Texas A&M students in grief.)

Source: Printed by permission of K. Fearn-Banks.

Vocabulary

bonfire tradition _____

_____

_____

_____

_____

Aggie Spirit _____

_____

_____

_____

_____

timeline _____

_____

_____

_____

_____

Critical Incidence Response Team _____

_____

_____

_____

_____

mock press conference _____

_____

_____

_____

_____

Chapter 9

Environmental Crisis

Case: Häagen-Dazs and the Honey Bees

Activities

1. Check out Häagen-Dazs containers and merchandise to see if there is information on the crisis aimed at consumers. Educating consumers and urging research are the two most important tactics until a way of protecting the honey bee is discovered.

2. Have other companies taken an active interest in this research?

Discussion and Essays

1. Häagen-Dazs has won numerous awards for its campaign, but, as of early 2010, the cause of the disappearance of the honey bee was still not known. Are there other tactics Häagen-Dazs could take on to alleviate the crisis?

2. Considering the foods impacted by honey bees, why do you think this crisis is not a major news event? What could make the news media more concerned about this issue?

3. What campaigns can be developed to further educate food stores that carry all foods threatened by the loss of the honey bee, not just ice creams and honey products?

4. How could social media be used to educate publics?

5. What courses and departments in colleges and universities should be concerned about this crisis?

6. What other companies or kinds of company have taken an active interest in this issue or this research?

Instructors: This case could lend itself to campus campaigns embracing several departments: environmental science, biology, culinary arts, nutrition, agriculture and farming, etc. It could also embrace the purpose of either educating campus or community publics about the problem, or helping to cope with some suspected causes of the decrease in the honey bee population. Or it might simply be a class group assignment to develop a campaign, starting with research (possibly in your geographical area), objectives, strategies, and culminating with either a plan for tactics or the actual performance of tactics. The chapter cites the following as probable causes of the bee crisis:

- parasites
- bacteria and disease
- virus
- pesticides or other chemicals.

Also possible:

- poor nutrition of bees
- contaminated water supply
- lack of genetic diversity and lineage of bees
- level of stress in adult bees (overcrowding, confinement)
- global warming.

Campus displays could be an exhibit of all the foods that will be missed should bees totally disappear. Grocery stores could be urged to cooperate. Displays could also show publics the difference between honey bees and other bees and encourage people to stop destroying honey bee hives.

The National American Pollinator Protection Campaign suggests creating pollinator-friendly habitats in backyards. Even children can get involved in this type of project (creating another public for a campaign). Information may be obtained from **www.pollinator.org**.

Vocabulary

cause-marketing campaign _____

_____

_____

_____

_____

_____

_____

Silver Anvil award _____
_____
_____
_____
_____
_____
_____

Chapter 10

Natural Disasters

Case: Hurricane Katrina and New Orleans

Hurricane Katrina was the greatest natural disaster to hit the United States when it attacked the Gulf States in August, 2005. The case study is primarily about the failure to communicate and the failure to heed prodromes (warning signs). Secondarily, it reflects efforts of various organizations to recover through communications.

Activities

1. Develop a communications plan for a natural disaster for your family.

2. How prepared are you for the most likely natural disaster in your area or state? Do you have an evacuation plan? How will your family members communicate with each other should they become separated? Don't count on cell phones.

3. If possible, have students develop a crisis plan for a disaster. Even if the university or college already has one, administrators might be interested in seeing what students would plan.

4. Check **nola.com** for blogs relating to Katrina recovery or later hurricane information.

5. Read the following reports (Boxes 10.1, 10.2, and 10.3) on the Red Cross in preparation for discussion and assignments.

Box 10.1 The Red Cross Charged with Overspending on Public Relations

February 29, 2006

The American Red Cross was under fire a few months after Hurricane Katrina for spending hundreds of thousands of dollars to boost its public image. The *Washington Post, Los Angeles Times*, and the Associated Press revealed that in 2004 and 2005, the Red Cross paid Public Strategies, a Houston corporate image agency, to brand chief executive officer Marsha Evans as the face of the Red Cross. The consultants were to secure at least two "media opportunities" per month for Evans and were to book her for public appearances before influential groups.

As the campaign continued, said the sources, the Red Cross was laying off workers in the blood-services operations. In its Washington, D.C. headquarters, employees' merit pay was eliminated and travel was limited. A Red Cross spokesperson said the consultants were instrumental in boosting donations when it booked appearances.

Evans had resigned about two months before the charges were made, citing differences with the 50-member Board of Governors.

During the same years, the organization paid nearly $114,000 to reach producers who would use the name of the charity in commercial television and film. Harvard University lecturer Peter Dobkin Hall, a specialist on non-profits, said the expenditure was not necessary. He said, "When disaster happens, people turn to the Red Cross and throw money at them!"

The world's largest charity was also charged with mismanagement of funds after the September 11 attacks. Then CEO Bernardine Healy resigned and the organization was warned to resolve its internal problem.

A board member, in 2001, warned Red Cross chairman David McLaughlin to resolve the group's disputes and said, "The worst thing we could do is to gloss over the split on the board . . . and see the whole scenario repeated 3 or 4 years from now." As he predicted, four years later, Hurricane Katrina hit and another CEO resigned.

(Data from *New York Times* Online)

Box 10.2 American Red Cross Volunteers Charged With Impropriety

March 24, 2006

John F. McGuire, interim president and chief executive of the American Red Cross, announced the organization had formed a team to investigate wide-ranging accusations of impropriety among volunteers during the Hurricane Katrina disaster.

The charges included improper division of relief supplies, use of felons as volunteers, the unauthorized possession of Red Cross computer equipment to manipulate databases, and the disappearance of rented cars, generators, and 3,000 to 9,000 air mattresses, among others.

Box 10.3 American Red Cross Fires Key Supervisors

March 25, 2006

The American Red Cross dismissed two key volunteer kitchen supervisors for improperly diverting relief supplies. Most, 95 percent, of Red Cross personnel are volunteers.

Among other improprieties, the supervisors were accused of ordering 1,500 meals per day for one New Orleans neighborhood when it was discovered that only 500 meals were needed.

(Data from *New York Times* Online)

Discussion and Essays

1. One of the strategies of the PR consultants in the first news story was getting Red Cross first-aid kits included in an episode of *The Real World* and Red Cross vehicles in an episode of *The West Wing*. The Red Cross received 60 percent of the $3.6 billion that Americans donated for hurricane relief. Millions of people saw these TV shows and the name of the American Red Cross. Was the money well spent? Should donor money be used on such efforts? What are the positives, and the negatives?

2. Read Peter Dobkin Hall's comment about the Red Cross in the first news story. If it is true, does the Red Cross need to do a public campaign in response to the charges? For giant disasters like September 11 and Hurricane Katrina, people did "throw money," but will they continue to donate for relatively small disasters when fewer people are impacted, when the news media coverage is not so massive?

3. Should the Red Cross just sit tight and let the charges die or initiate a campaign to save or boost its reputation? Visualize such a campaign.

Other Reports

Box 10.4 Choose Your Disaster and Be Prepared

No matter where you live in the United States, you can expect a natural disaster. Hurricanes, from June to November, generally strike the states bordering the Atlantic and the Gulf of Mexico. Earthquakes, tsunamis, and volcanic eruptions are expected in the Pacific Coast states, including Alaska, as well as other cities. Tornadoes, from late spring to early summer, touch ground in Midwestern states. Blizzards, between December and April, fall on northern states, except for Washington and Oregon. Flash floods generally occur in Texas, New Mexico, Arizona, Colorado, South Dakota, and Kentucky. Many people die in big city heat waves in the eastern half of the country during summer, and to a lesser degree in hot western states and rural areas. Wildfires generally affect the western half of the United States.

Then, there are Nor'easters in the Northeastern states, river valley flooding in the northern Midwest states, and lightning strikes and thunderstorms in most states other than the western states.

Of all states, Nevada is least likely to suffer a natural disaster and Texas is most likely.

(Data from *USA Today*, April 20, 2006, p. 7D)

Box 10.5 Students from New Orleans Colleges Learn an Unplanned Lesson

Colleges and universities in New Orleans had to close abruptly after the Hurricane Katrina disaster. Tulane, Dillard, Loyola, Xavier, and Southern University, New Orleans were the primary institutions of higher education damaged. Students were scattered at universities all over the U.S. Hundreds of faculty were cut. Some tenured faculty were urged to consider retirement. Damage to the campus and buildings was extensive. When classes resumed in 2006, housing was a challenge and some grad programs were cut. Some opportunities were created. Courses ranging from engineering to sociology were built on the hurricane's aftermath at Tulane. Students at Dillard already were required to complete 120 hours of community service, and had to complete a Katrina-related academic project.

(Data from the Associated Press, January 16, 2006)

Discussion and Essays

1. What gains could students achieve from the experience?

2. If your campus was devastated by a natural disaster, where would you relocate temporarily?

3. What classes not taught now could be developed to take advantage of the disaster experience?

4. In the areas of communications and journalism, how could students expand learning? Should some of these classes be offered anyway?

5. Does your college or university offer classes resulting from the September 11 tragedies, or Hurricane Katrina, or the Oklahoma bombing?

6. What image do you recall most from the disaster?

7. Do people react more to imagery or words?

8. What segments of the public were not given information about methods of evacuation?

9. Why would looters steal televisions in a city where there is no electricity and no people?

Vocabulary

Vonage Internet phone _____

_____

_____

_____

_____

refugee _____

_____

_____

_____

_____

looter _____

_____

_____

_____

_____

global warming _____

_____

_____

_____

_____

Federal Emergency Management Agency (FEMA) _____

_____

_____

_____

_____

nola.com _____

_____

_____

_____

_____

mulatto _____

_____

_____

_____

_____

quadroon _____

_____

_____

_____

_____

octoroon _____

_____

_____

_____

_____

ham radio _____

_____

_____

_____

_____

MRE (meals ready to eat) _____

_____

_____

_____

_____

Chapter 11

Transportation Crises

Case: Holland America Line and Cruise Crises

Activity

1. This chapter illustrates the vast numbers of crises one company can encounter. Using any company or business—local, national, or international—list crises it *could* suffer.

Discussion and Essays

1. Pick a possible preventable crisis in a local company and discuss how a campaign could be developed to prevent the occurrence. (Check Chapter 15, The Crisis Communications Plan.)

2. What could be done to prevent non-expert experts from giving false information to the news media? If you were a TV news reporter covering a crisis on a ship, from what source would you seek information? Who would you trust for accurate information? Who would provide the most interesting information, the quotes that bring good ratings? If this presents a dilemma for you, what are the pros and cons of the issue?

3. Looking at local businesses, what companies have had prodromes warning them of possible crises?

4. If the bungee jumper had been killed, or even worse, if he had fallen on a passenger causing injury or death, would the cruise ship bear any responsibility? Would the name of the ship end up in the headlines or leads of news stories? Would that affect the reputation of the cruise company and affect future travelers?

5. How would you feel if you were on a ship that went off course to assist a stranded fishing boat and the deed caused you to lose a visit to a port? Would you demand a refund or wait for the cruise line to offer a settlement?

6.   If a cruise ship is near the site of a terrorist attack or a crime wave, should the captain inform passengers even if he is certain there is no danger to the ship or its passengers? Would that cause panic? If you think the captain should deliver the information to passengers, how should he—by public address system, by in-person meetings, by newsletter?

Vocabulary

incident command center _____

_____

_____

_____

_____

rescue coordination center _____

_____

_____

_____

_____

Case: US Airways and the Emergency Landing in the Hudson

Activities

Figure 11.1 was the first news release distributed by the US Airways corporate communications team. Its goal was to send out additional news releases every 15 minutes as information developed. Notice it includes all the elements below for News Release #1. Write the second and third updates to include the indicated information.

- **News Release #1:** Initial report. Flight number, aircraft type, O&D (origin and destination), location of accident, time, time zone, airline's concern, advice to family members, what US Airways is doing.

- **Update #2:** Includes initial report information, adds crew information (two pilots, three flight attendants were on board). The plane was supposed to leave LaGuardia at 2:45, but left at 3:03 Eastern Time. The US Airways Care team of specially trained employee volunteers to assist families and passengers has been activated.

- **Update #3:** Includes number of passengers (150) plus all information on previous releases.

US Airways Flight 1549 Initial Report

Tempe, Ariz.—(Business Wire)—Jan. 15, 2009—US Airways (NYSE: LCC) flight 1549, an Airbus A320 en route to Charlotte from LaGuardia, has been involved in an accident in New York approximately 3:03 p.m. Eastern Time.

Airline officials are in direct contact with local, state, and national authorities and are cooperating fully with emergency response efforts. US Airways' primary concern at this time is for those on board the airplane and their families.

US Airways is confirming passengers and crew on board the aircraft and will issue additional information as soon as possible. At this point, no additional details can be confirmed.

Individuals who believe they may have family members on board flight 1549 may call US Airways at 1–800–679–8215 within the United States. This number can be reached toll-free from international locations though AT&T's USADirect®. To contact an AT&T operator, please visit **www.usa.com/traveler** for USADirect® access codes.

US Airways will provide additional information as it becomes available. Please monitor usairways.com for the latest information. (LCCG).

—LCC—

CONTACT:

US Airways

Media Relations, 480–693–5729

Figure 11.1 US Airways Press Release. This was the first news release distributed by the US Airways corporate communications team. Its goal was to send out additional news releases every 15 minutes as information developed.

Source: US Airways.

Discussion and Essays

1.   Factual or first? Is it better for a communications team to come forward with information first, or wait to get each fact confirmed before releasing it? What are the difficulties each way?

2.   Crisis communications plans need to be both concise and complete. James Olson, when he took over as vice president, corporate communications, at US Airways, inherited a cumbersome crisis communications plan—125 pages and numerous updates by predecessors over the years. It wasn't "user friendly." What elements of a plan must be updated regularly? Consider the plans in the appendices of the textbook and the elements of a plan in Chapter 15.

3.   This "good news" crisis was nearly as much work for the corporate communications team as a "bad news" crisis would have been, perhaps surprisingly so?

4.   After Captain Sullenberger landed the plane safely in the Hudson River, he became a celebrity. What does this incident say about crises presenting opportunity?

5.   Notice that the staff members of the corporate communications team left vacations and other engagements immediately to head to assigned stations from which they would get to work on the crisis response. These actions are carefully planned and should be arranged for any crisis at any company. Each person has a duty and knows what he/she must do. Some organizations have plans so tight that team members can get to the command center within an hour of notification. Discuss this planning and what effort must go into it. What exceptions might there be to being present at the command center? Backups? How can this be practiced?

Chapter 12

Product Failure and Product Tampering

Case: Yuhan-Kimberly and Baby Wet Wipes

Activities

1. Write a news release using the information in the "standby statement" issued online by Yuhan-Kimberly. (See Box 12.1, p. 68.)

2. Check websites for U.S. manufacturers of wet wipes and similar products and see if any safety issues or safety standards are mentioned.

Other Cases of Product Failure: Perrier, Pillsbury, and Beech-Nut

Perrier—trusted and respected for its pure, fresh, sparkling water from a French spring—learned in 1990 that its scare was actually a problem with its product. There were traces of a cancer-causing substance called benzene found in a bottle of Perrier. It turned out not to be a case of malicious tampering; a faulty filter was to blame.

The company recalled 70 million bottles, suffered a loss of sales amounting to $40 million, and paid an additional $25 million (in advertising, public relations, etc.) to recover from the crisis.

In 1984, Pillsbury found ethylene dibromide (EDB), also a carcinogen, in several of its products made from grains. It pulled the products. The move cost millions of dollars in lost sales and staff hours of employees, not to mention embarrassment.

Beech-Nut was caught in an embarrassing situation when the federal government charged that it defrauded and misled consumers by saying it made 100 percent apple juice, when actually the juice contained various other products, but very little apple juice.

Beech-Nut paid a $2 million fine and $140,000 in investigative costs to the FDA. Beech-Nut's president pleaded guilty to 10 counts of violating the Food, Drug, and Cosmetic Act and was given a $100,000 fine, as well as a period of probation.

The Beech-Nut, Pillsbury, and Perrier cases turned out to be "product failure" crises. Such crises can be quite different from "product tampering" crises, such as the Tylenol crisis and the Diet Pepsi syringes-in-the-can scares.

Box 12.1 Yuhan-Kimberly Wet Wipes Are Safe!

In the developed countries such as United States, EU, etc., the generic product wet wipes is classified as cosmetics and its quality and safety are rigorously controlled by administration than any other industrial products. Here, the maximum permissible level of formaldehyde in cosmetics is 2,000 ppm.

Use of formaldehyde in the local cosmetics is also allowed by 2,000 ppm just like United States, EU, Canada and Australia. With much reinforced quality and safety control than regulation, Yuhan-Kimberly's Baby Wet Wipes has become the most loved one over the past 5 years.

According to the recent examination of one consumer organization, 210 ppm of formaldehyde was detected in the Yuhan-Kimberly's Baby Wet Wipes. As noted before, this amount is only 1/10 of both local and other developed countries' regulation, and it had been reconfirmed as being safe. However, the consumer organization asked the local companies to adjust the amount not exceeding 30 ppm once in the past, which falls into the guideline for the 'voluntary safety mark' of the Wet Wipes.

Though Yuhan-Kimberly is convinced of the safety of Baby Wet Wipes, we decided to accept return or exchange products, with respecting the 'voluntary safety mark' guideline. The consumer who is currently using the product can either keep it or replace.

Separately, we will closely work with the related organizations to close the gap between 2000 ppm, which is the common regulation in both of the developed countries' and the local cosmetics, and 30 ppm, which is the 'voluntary safety mark' guideline.

(This is a news release translated into English by Yuhan-Kimberly executives. Courtesy of Yuhan-Kimberly.)

Discussion and Essays

1. Compare and contrast failure crises, including recent crises not in the textbook.

2. Why do you think this was a problem in Korea and not in other Asian countries, in Europe, or in the United States? Do U.S. consumers trust manufacturers to provide safe products because of government regulations?

3. How do you think the Korean culture might affect the attitudes of parents in this crisis? The Yuhan-Kimberly spokesman revealed that parents in Korea often have only one child, ideally no more than two. This is a choice; there are no laws governing the number of children in Korea. Parents only have the number of children they feel they can afford. If parents have only one child, are they more protective of that child than if they have two or three or four?

4. The Yuhan-Kimberly crisis began online and was fought online. If parents in the United States objected on blogs to a similar problem, what could crisis communicators do to ensure that the safety of babies is not compromised? What methods of communications would be most effective? What would be key messages? Any special events or special promotions? If the issue originated on blogs, would you limit the campaign to online communications, or would you also seek the news media? If the complaints were limited to one city, would you respond only in that city?

5. What did the spokesman mean when he said, in his conclusion, "Approach with a human face is the basic part of crisis communication" (see textbook page 243)?

Vocabulary

standby statement _____

_____

_____

_____

_____

corporate social responsibility _____

_____

_____

_____

_____

Case: Maple Leaf Foods and the Battle Against Listeria

Activities

1. Incidents of product failure occur frequently. Compare and contrast responses of newer cases with the response of Maple Leaf.

2. Compare Maple Leaf's crisis communications in 2008 with Johnson & Johnson's (Chapter 7) in 1982. How are responses different and similar? How are corporate and communications ideologies different and similar?

3. Check **mapleleaf.com** to see if there are newer safety precautions or changes.

Discussion and Essays

1. Compare and contrast CEOs in various cases in the textbook.

2. The Maple Leaf crisis was not front-page news in the United States. But why should U.S. companies using meat slicers be well aware of the crisis?

3. Online, CEO McCain is the only spokesperson visible to the public. Is that a good move (externally and internally), and why?

4. Is a video news release of a CEO or spokesperson making an explanation or an apology more effective in impressing consumers than having them read the actual speech? If so, what makes it more effective? If not, why? Does the spokesperson's appearance (body size, facial features, hair, clothing, facial expressions) make a difference? If appearance matters, reconsider the first part of this question—if the CEO is not physically attractive, is the video speech or the written speech more effective? What does this tell us about training spokespersons?

5. Maple Leaf said it released fact sheets of new safety procedures, backgrounders explaining progress. Other than its website and the news media, to whom did the company send these?

6. The fact was disseminated that 5 percent of humans carry listeria in their intestines without ill effects. Does using this fact make the company seem less responsible? Does it seem like an excuse? Should the company cite even more information about listeria as a common disease?

Case: Wendy's and the Finger-in-the-Chili Hoax

This case study shows how one greedy customer's hoax affected a large restaurant chain and how it worked with law enforcement, the news media, and its consumer public to recover.

Activity

Write a statement for *Good Morning America* explaining Wendy's position, but without showing anger for the woman who started the hoax and without saying in specific words that she is a liar.

Another Tampering Case: Coors Beer

Perhaps the most ridiculous tampering crisis was the one Coors suffered in 1988. A Jacksonville, Florida, man claimed that he had found a mouse in his beer can.

Coors offered the man $1,500 for the can containing the mouse, but the man tried to barter for $50,000. Coors refused, so he went to the media and succeeded in getting a piece on the WTLV-TV evening news. All of Jacksonville could see the mouse fall out of the can and imagine drinking a can of beer with a mouse in it. Consequently, a quarter of a million dollars was lost in sales, but, fortunately for Coors, the incident did not become a national crisis.

Coors ordered laboratory tests on the mouse and learned that the mouse had been dead only a week, whereas the can it was in was sealed three months before. Also, the mouse did not drown; it was killed by being stuffed into the can's pop-top opening.

Even though the case was obviously a tampering case, and even though the man was prosecuted, the film news footage aired 72 times in the Jacksonville area. A long time passed before many beer drinkers could pick up a can of Coors.

Discussion and Essays

1. How are the Coors and Wendy's cases similar and different?

2. This case was a crisis for Wendy's because of a vicious act by a customer. What actions would a restaurant take if similar charges were true? The Associated Press, on May 2, 2006, wrote of a diner in the TGI Friday's in College Mall, Indiana, who found a piece of human flesh on his hamburger. A restaurant worker had accidentally cut his finger and did not realize a piece of his finger was gone until after he arrived at a hospital for treatment. The diner reported the incident to police, who told him it was not a criminal matter.

3. What should TGI Friday's do? What arrangement should/could be made with the customer? Should an announcement be made to the public? If so, what should be said? Will such an announcement attract more attention than ignoring the incident and letting it die? What should be done internally?

4. What excellence model did the crisis team follow most closely?

5. What publics did the communications department deal with most closely? What other publics were important?

6. How did the Wendy's crisis plan follow the image restoration theory?

7. If the Wendy's team members had not been as sure that Wendy's was not at fault, how would they have altered the way they approached the crisis? This question is a bit different from the TGI Friday's story. That company knew it was guilty.

8. How can Wendy's turn the crisis into an opportunity?

9. What other crises might Wendy's battle?

10. Other than free Frostys, what else could Wendy's do to get customers to return?

Mini-Case: Domino's

Discussion and Essays

1. Discuss the pros and cons of battling a crisis online only versus using more traditional communications methods. The video was only seen online, so would extending the battle to newspapers and television inform and disgust people who never knew of the prank? Would this cause those people to refrain from buying Domino's products? Should Domino's have saturated all media to get its viewpoint out?

Chapter 13

Death and Injury

Case: Columbine High School and the Shooting Tragedy

Activities

An online game called "Super Columbine Massacre RPG" was posted on a website in 2005. It includes images of the two students, Dylan Klebold and Eric Harris, who killed 12 classmates and a teacher at Columbine High School. Players of the game determine how many people Klebold and Harris kill on any given day. Every time someone is killed, a dialogue box pops up that reads, "Another victory for the Trench Coat Mafia." There are also images, but not photographs, of students running from the crime scene.

The site's creator told the *Rocky Mountain News*, "I was a bullied kid. I didn't fit in and I was surrounded by a culture of elitism as espoused by our school's athletes." He also said he hoped the game would "promote a real dialogue on the subject of school shootings."

The father of one of the Columbine victims said, "It disgusts me. You trivialize the actions of two murderers and the lives of the innocent." A student left paralyzed after the shooting said, ". . . overall, I got the feeling it might be helpful in some ways. I don't think it's bad to discuss."

Discussion and Essays

1. Imagine such a game. What do you think of this game? Is it insensitive, does it trivialize the actions of killers, or would it serve as a prodrome to those who play it, urging them to heed warning signs? How could an online game about the incident be made to be a lesson of understanding? Can a game be fun and educational/informative?

2. San Francisco psychologist Mark Zaslav was quoted in the *Seattle Post-Intelligencer* (April 2, 2006, page F1) as saying the following:

   Research shows that people who go on to commit violent acts generally display serious psychiatric maladjustment relatively early. Features such as deficits in the capacity for empathy, absence of mature prosocial guilt for suffering caused to others, idiosyncratic violent fantasies and behavior, cruelty to animals, classmates or siblings, low tolerance for frustration, excessive anger, and substance abuse are often in evidence long before the culminating violent act. Parental abuse, neglect or other trauma may occasionally figure in the picture. Each case is different and human behavior is complex, but in short, "gentle," "normal," people generally do not commit mass murder.

Considering Zaslav's comments, why are mass murderers often depicted in the news media as shocking those who knew them with sudden violent behavior? Reporters frequently quote mothers and friends who say, "The person I know couldn't possibly have killed anyone. He was too gentle, too sweet." Are parents and friends suffering from shock and grief good subjects for investigations into why a crime is committed? On the other hand, are victims' families and friends more reliable sources? Who would be a good source?

3. After the Columbine shooting, a $1.5 million memorial honoring the 13 people slain was proposed to be constructed in a park near the school. It will include a water fountain and a station for each victim, with messages from their families engraved on an outer ring. In June 2006, former President Bill Clinton attended the ceremonial groundbreaking and announced that he would donate $50,000 to the project. About $250,000 was then needed. Clinton also attended a 2004 fundraiser. Activity: Prepare a timeline of events leading up to the construction and opening/dedication of the memorial. Include steps backwards, such as time spent to raze the library where most victims were killed and the economic downturn after the September 11 tragedies, when the projected cost was lowered from $2.5 million. This activity could also be (especially after the memorial is erected) a timeline of what has happened at every anniversary of the shooting.

4. In Pennsylvania, in May 2006, an 18-year-old youth, disturbed because his girlfriend left him, was found in a school stairwell with bottle rockets, a loaded rifle, and a hunting knife. The school principal and others talked him into surrendering. He said he was thinking of "ending it all." In Puyallup, Washington, in April 2006, a 16-year-old said he had planned to use a handgun and randomly kill 15 classmates, then save the last round for himself.

After a near-incident, what crisis communications should be disseminated from the school or school district to the following: (1) students, (2) parents, (3) community members? Should any of these communications be disseminated even if there have been no prodromes?

Case: Metro Transit: Driver Shot, Bus Flies Off a Bridge

Discussion and Essays

1. The spokespersons for Metro Transit, the hospitals, the police department, and the fire department agreed at the site of the accident to answer media questions related to their specific areas. They could have made that decision prior to the crisis. As major city or county agencies, one could assume in pre-crisis planning that they would be involved in a bus accident and violent crime. What could the spokespersons have known about each other even before the crisis that would have helped make the communications process more effective?

2. The news media, for the most part, sympathized with Metro Transit. If the media had been combative and aggressive, how might the outcome of the crisis have been different?

3. An excerpt from a *Seattle Post-Intelligencer* news story published nearly a year after the bus tragedy is reprinted in Figure 13.1. What questions might a reporter ask to complete the story? What information was probably included in the rest of the story?

4. Which questions would be aimed at the Metro Transit spokesperson? Which questions would be asked of other persons? Why isn't the bus driver's name mentioned in the story? Do you think it was the reporter's decision alone, or was she influenced by Metro Transit?

5. According to Table 13.1, Metro Transit routes 7 and 174 were the most dangerous to drivers and passengers in 1998. There were 11 bus routes overall with assaults in the first 11 months of 1998. These routes also had the most passengers. The assaults ranged from fare disputes and evasions to the 1998 shooting. Planning a campaign to communicate with riders on various routes is an example of segmenting publics. Other than through news-media coverage, how could Metro Transit persuade riders of routes 7 and 174 of improved bus safety?

6. Should Metro Transit plan a communications program for passengers riding Routes 307 and 42? Why, or why not?

Vocabulary

police radio scanner _____

_____

_____

_____

_____

soft news _____

_____

_____

_____

_____

media relations technology _____

_____

_____

_____

_____

Metro Driver Attacked by Woman With Knife

A routine morning commute ended in bloodshed yesterday when a veteran Metro Transit bus driver was stabbed by a passenger wielding a paring knife and ranting about demons and sunspots.

The woman, who was later arrested, attacked the 53-year-old driver before 9 a.m. as he ferried passengers from downtown Seattle to Queen Anne Hill.

As the bus turned into Broad Street from Third Avenue, the unruly rider stood and shouted, distracting the driver and other passengers.

"The passenger was creating a disturbance and annoying the other passengers, but the driver didn't have any sense that she was dangerous," said Metro spokesman Dan Williams.

When the driver warned her to sit down or get off, the woman screamed: "I'll kill you and I'll drive the bus myself!" Then she lunged at the driver.

As he struggled to control the moving bus, stunned passengers watched the woman jab a 3-inch knife into the driver's left hand . . .

Figure 13.1 An excerpt from a news story written by Kimberly A. C. Wilson in the *Seattle Post-Intelligencer* on November 19, 1999, one year after the 1998 Metro Transit shooting and accident that left the bus driver, the assailant, and a passenger dead.

Table 13.1 Number of Assaults on Metro Transit Buses During an 11-Month Period in 1998 (injury and non-injury assaults)[a]

	Against drivers			Against passengers		
Route	Injury Assaults	Non-injury Assaults	Total Driver Assaults	Injury Assaults	Non-injury Assaults	Total Passenger Assaults
7	1	6	7	4	22	26
174	2	3	5	8	19	27
6	3	2	5	3	12	15
359[b]	1	3	4	0	2	2
36	1	3	4	2	7	9
150	2	2	4	1	6	7
106	0	4	4	0	7	7
21	0	2	2	4	1	5
42	0	0	0	0	2	2
307	0	2	2	0	1	1
48	0	3	3	0	4	4

a Some "non-injury assaults" included refusals to pay fares.
b Express version of route 6.

Source: Data from King County Metro Transit, 1998.

Chapter 14

Individuals in Crises

Activities

1. Explore how actors, sports figures, and political figures are perceived in other countries. In Korea, for example, celebrities are more accountable to the people than in the United States. Athletes from other countries in the 2010 winter Olympics in Vancouver spoke about how they were seeking to please their fellow citizens, whereas U.S. athletes' primary goals seemed to be individual medals and lucrative advertising contracts.

2. Choose recent scandals of celebrities and discuss whether they reacted well or not so well. What would you have advised them to do differently?

Discussion and Essays

1. How do you feel about the behavior of celebrities? Do you care that their personal life is not idyllic? Do you believe they owe it to the people who buy sports tickets, movie tickets, concert tickets, vote in elections, or watch television, to lead an admirable life? If so, do you refrain from supporting celebrities when they fail you, or do you easily forgive and/or forget? Do you feel comforted that noted people have the same problems as "regular people?" Do you seek celebrities on fan pages, websites, and blogs? If so, why? How do you feel about an actor who is excellent on screen or onstage, but you know nothing about his or her personal life? Is that OK?

2. When celebrities violate social standards or laws, if they apologize, seemingly sincerely, are you satisfied?

3. Do you think celebrities should go to jail if they commit crimes, major or minor? Paris Hilton's days in jail were catastrophic to her, but critics say they were slaps on the wrist compared with the sentences of "real people." Is that situation as it should be? Should wealth and fame affect outcome?

4. Why do political figures frequently lose their positions after scandals, but entertainers and sports figures, even if they go to jail, are often returned to their former positions as stars? If you were a publicist or agent to a celebrity, would you attempt to establish rules with your client, warn him/her about appropriate and inappropriate behavior, or just bank your salary and let things occur?

5. Do you think the news media should keep silent when they know some celebrities are in trouble? If so, how and why?

6. Political scandals in the U.S. have existed as long as the U.S. is old. Why are some well known and talked about and others are relatively hidden?

7. Only a few years ago, tabloid newspapers were the only press that covered salacious scandals. Now, nearly all the news media do. Why this turn? Is this going to be true always? Will the news media get bored with cheating scandals and stop covering them?

8. Recently, celebrities in spousal cheating scandals have been said to have retreated to sex rehabilitation clinics. Do they really seek treatment, or is it the illusion of getting treatment that they seek?

9. Do more male celebrities than female have extramarital affairs? Do you believe there are women who have affairs with celebrities to make themselves popular and admired by their circle of acquaintances, or even to achieve a measure of fame themselves?

Vocabulary

apology _____

_____

_____

_____

transparency (transparent) _____

_____

_____

_____

translucency (translucent) _____

_____

_____

_____

opacity (opaque) _____

_____

_____

_____

The Crisis Communications Plan

Chapter 15 primarily outlines a step-by-step procedure for developing a Crisis Communications Plan.

Crisis Inventory

To determine an organization's most likely crises, the public relations department, with key executives, must take an inventory. A sample graph showing how crises are plotted and a blank graph for you to plot your own plan are provided in Figures 15.1 and 15.2 on pages 105 and 106, respectively. Each possible crisis must be ranked as follows:

0—Impossible; that is, the crisis has basically no chance of occurring

1—Nearly impossible

2—Remote to possible

3—Possible

4—More than possible, somewhat probable; has happened to competitors or similar companies

5—Highly probable; may or may not have previously occurred in the company, but warning signs are evident

Each crisis also should be ranked according to its potential damage to the company. The rankings in this category are as follows:

0—No damage, not a serious consequence

1—Little damage, can be handled without much difficulty, not serious enough for the media's concern

2—Some damage, a slight chance that the media will be involved

3—Considerable damage, but still will not be a major media issue

4—Considerable damage, would definitely be a major media issue

5—Devastating, front-page news, could put the company out of business

For added security, when in doubt rank a crisis in the next highest category. For instance, Company Z may identify five crises that it could face: workplace violence, fire, protest demonstrations, negative legislation, and tax problems. Each of these crises might be ranked as shown in Table 15.1 on page 117.

After rankings for probability and damage are made, bar graphs should be made to clearly show each crisis so it can be compared with others. At the base of a blank graph, write the name of each type of crisis (see Figure 15.1). Plot the height of each bar according to numbers attributed to each crisis in the probability and damage rankings. Choose different colors or shadings for probability bars and damage bars.

When Company Z plots its data on a bar graph, it resembles Figure 15.1. Considering Company Z's graph, we see that the probability and seriousness of a crisis relating to tax problems are not as crucial as those of the other crises. Negative legislation, although a very likely crisis, seems not to be particularly critical. On the other hand, protest demonstrations are critical, although not very likely. Workplace violence and fire seem both likely and critical.

Most organizations plan for crises ranked high in both probability and damage. In this case, Company Z would probably develop crisis management and communications plans for workplace violence first, then for the other crises in descending order of importance: fire, protest demonstrations, negative legislation, and tax problems.

Sometimes, organizations make crisis plans for the most devastating crises, no matter how probable or improbable they may be. In this case, Company Z would develop plans for workplace violence first, followed by protest demonstrations, then fire. Some organizations use 10 instead of 5 for measuring degrees of probability and damage. Still, 10 would be the highest probability or damage, and one would be the lowest.

The importance of the crisis inventory is to force organizations to think about the possibilities. The ranking procedure may introduce ideas for prevention programs. You also may realize that your organization is more vulnerable than you anticipated.

Crisis Inventory Results

The accompanying crisis inventory graph analyzes five possible crises that could occur at UDUB's Burger Drive-In: *E. coli* poisoning, hepatitis A, fire, injury, and violence. By studying the probability of each possible crisis and the amount of possible damage that could result if that crisis occurred, it was determined that UDUB's Burger Drive-In is most vulnerable to the crises involving *E. coli* and hepatitis A outbreaks. Hence, this crisis plan was created to suit the needs of UDUB's Burger Drive-In in case one of these emergencies should occur.

Developing the Crisis Communications Plan

In the event that you develop a Crisis Communications Plan as a class project or as an independent project, the following pages take you step by step through the process. If you do not intend to do a plan, turn to the exercise on page 104.

Before you draft a plan, you must first determine what crisis or crises the plan is intended to manage. You may develop one plan for various crises in which only certain pages will be different, or you may have different plans for different crises.

This activity is designed for one crisis. In order to use this section of the workbook effectively, it is suggested that a potential crisis be selected and followed throughout—for example, a hurricane, a flood, a fire, or food poisoning in the dorms. The crisis selected will make a difference in the compiling of lists and, of course, in the drafting of messages.

Step 1: Design the Cover Page

Write the title for the crisis communications plan—for example, "Crisis Communications Plan for Campus Violence at . . ." Include the following:

- The names of the person(s) writing the plan
- The date when the plan was written
- The dates when the plan was tested.

Write a draft of the cover page. An example is shown in Box 15.1.

Step 2: Write the Introduction

Ask the head of the company to answer the following questions (or ask a PR professional to ghostwrite the answers):

- Why is this plan important?
- What can happen if it is not followed?
- Have there been warning signs?
- Has the crisis happened before here?
- Has it happened to similar organizations?

The message should be persuasive and encouraging. A table of contents should precede the introduction and acknowledgments. Box 15.2 shows a sample introduction.

Step 3: Prepare Acknowledgments

Have key executives and key personnel in the plan sign this affidavit, verifying that they have read the plan and are prepared to put it into effect. See Box 15.3 for an example.

Box 15.1 UDUB Burger Drive-In's Crisis Communications Plan for *E. coli* and Hepatitis A

Crisis Communications Plan Team
School of Communications
University of Washington
Professor Kathleen Fearn-Banks

Written March 10, 2008

Dana Anderson

Jennifer Boyeson

Sarah Doran

Meg Hemphill

Stacy Jaffe

Melissa Jones

Jaime Kennerud

David Masin

Alexandra Ootkin

Danielle Rosenow

Julie Sanders

Diva Sze

Revised May 25, 2009

Sarah Doran

Meg Hemphill

Melissa Jones

Jaime Kennerud

Danielle Rosenow

Tested: _____

_____

_____

Box 15.2 A Sample Statement From Management to Employees

There are many high-risk factors surrounding the food industry, making it necessary for all food organizations to be ready for a potential crisis at any time. Our risks are heightened by the nature of our industry: We provide quick and simple food service. Especially with meat, there is a high risk of food poisoning if the meat is not cooked properly. Because of these dangers, it is vital that UDUB Burger's employees are prepared to deal with the media and the public quickly and efficiently in the event of a crisis.

We have worked for many years to build an impeccable reputation with the public by providing clean, quick, and quality service and food to our consumers. Because the most damaging scare in the food industry, particularly with hamburgers, is food poisoning—particularly the *E. coli* virus and hepatitis A—it is crucial that UDUB Burger be prepared for any possible circumstances involving a patron of our restaurant becoming ill from our food. The *E. coli* crisis that struck Jack-in-the-Box was a warning sign to all fast-food handlers. In order to prevent similar damage to our company, we must take very seriously what happened at Jack-in-the-Box and what Foodmaker did wrong in communicating with the media and the public.

If this plan is not followed in the event of a crisis, irreparable damage to the reputation of UDUB Burger Drive-In is possible. The loss of trust among our consumers could also lead to a large loss of business. In dealing with this crisis plan, we must keep in mind that trust and reliability are incredibly important to consumers when choosing a place to eat, and UDUB Burger must protect its reputation as being a reliable fast-food source. We trust you will all keep up the outstanding work in order to protect our company from such a crisis.

Box 15.3 Sample Acknowledgment

By signing this statement, I verify that I have read this plan and am prepared to put it into effect.

President and CEO   _____
                          (Signature and date)

Vice President and CFO   _____
                          (Signature and date)

Vice President   _____
                          (Signature and date)

Office Manager   _____
                          (Signature and date)

Step 4: Sample Rehearsal Dates Schedule

List the dates when the crisis plan was rehearsed (at least once or twice each year). Example:

Box 15.4 Sample Rehearsal Dates Schedule

Rehearsal Dates   June 24, 2008

Dec. 12, 2008

_____

_____

Step 5: The Purpose and Objectives of the Plan

Keeping a specific crisis in mind, state the purpose and objectives of the plan, including the company's overall policy on communications. Box 15.5 shows an example from the UDUB Burger Crisis Communications Plan.

Step 6: List Key Publics

In a format most convenient to the organization, list all key publics—both external and internal. You should probably rank them in order from most important to least important. The list should be comprehensive, including all publics and stakeholders with whom the organization must communicate during the crisis. Not every public needs to be notified in each crisis, but the list should be comprehensive. Unneeded publics can be eliminated at the time of the crisis.

All methods of reaching these stakeholders should be listed: office phone, home phone, car and cell phone, e-mail, neighbors, parents, vacation homes, clubs, and so on. If people check Facebook more often than other means of communications, use Facebook, or whatever social media they may use.

Notice the checklists for various media in Figures 15.9–15.10 on pages 114–116. Your lists may take this form. You may decide to compile several other lists, such as a city government list, a county government list, a state list, and a federal list. Maybe few or none of these apply to your organization. Develop the lists that are pertinent to you. Remember that, if there are serious injuries or damages, officials not normally concerned with your organization will be very much concerned.

Boxes 15.6–15.9 list key publics and include information on how to notify them of crucial information.

Box 15.5 Sample Purpose and Objectives Statement

PURPOSE

In the event of an *E. coli* or hepatitis A outbreak, we must take immediate action to inform our publics of the situation and the measures they need to take. Our open and honest transfer of information to the media and health care facilities will eliminate confusion among our publics. If we are truthful and forthright, the crisis situation can be more smoothly resolved and action can be taken to eliminate any future problems.

OBJECTIVES

We will make every effort to:

1. Initiate the Crisis Communications Plan within 2 hours.

2. Inform all health care organizations that might be involved with the situation.

3. Inform all owners and managers within 3 hours of the outbreak.

4. Inform the media and restaurant patrons within 4 hours of the outbreak.

5. Keep the media and all publics regularly informed of updated information.

6. Maintain honesty with the media about all known information.

7. Find the source of the problem as soon as possible.

8. Distribute our findings to the media and all publics.

9. Develop ways to alleviate future problems.

10. Implement necessary changes as soon as possible and resume business as usual.

Box 15.6 Sample List of Key Publics

LOCAL TELEVISION NEWS PERSONNEL

Station/ Channel	Address	News Director	Phone	Fax
KCTS/9	401 Mercer St. Seattle, WA 98109	Jane Sheridan	_____	_____
KING/5	333 Dexter Ave. N. Seattle, WA 98109	Eric Lerner Ron Taylor (weekend)	_____ _____	_____ _____
KIRO/7	2807 3rd Ave. Seattle, WA 98121	Bill Lord Tim Smith Assignment editor	_____ _____	_____ _____
KOMO/4	100 4th Ave. Seattle, WA 98121	Joe Barnes Paula Marimon (weekend)	_____ _____	_____ _____
KSTW/11	P.O. Box 1141 Seattle, WA 98411	Dan Ackler Keith Groteluchen (weekend ed.)	_____ _____	_____ _____
KCPQ/13	1813 Westlake Ave. N. Seattle, WA 98109	Todd Mokhtari Cory Bertman (managing editor)	_____ _____	_____ _____

Box 15.7 Sample List of Key Publics

LOCAL RADIO NEWS PERSONNEL

Station/ Channel	Address	News Director	Phone	Fax
KING/ 1090AM	333 Dexter Ave. N. Seattle, WA 98109	Tony Miner	_____	_____
KIRO/710AM	2807 3rd Ave. Seattle, WA 98121	Gail Neubert	_____	_____
KPLU/88FM	121 St. & Park Ave. Seattle, WA 98447	Michael Marcotte	_____	_____
KUOW/94FM	Univ. of WA Seattle, WA 98195	Marcie Stillman	_____	_____
KOMO/ 1000AM	100 4th Ave. Seattle, WA 98121	Jennifer Beschel	_____	_____

Box 15.8 Sample List of Key Publics

LOCAL NEWSPAPER PERSONNEL

Newspaper	Address	Phone/Fax	When/ Frequency
Seattle Times City Editor: Bill Ristow	P.O. Box 70 Seattle, WA 98111	_____	P.M., daily
Morning News Editor: Tom Osborne	P.O. Box 1100 Tacoma, WA 98411	_____	A.M., daily
Everett Herald Editor: Sam Strick	P.O. Box 930 Everett, WA 98206	_____	P.M., daily
American Journal	1705 132nd Ave. NE Bellevue, WA 98005	_____	P.M., daily
Eastside Week Editor: Pricilla Turner	123 Lake St. Kirkland, WA 98035	_____	A.M., weekly
Seattle Weekly Editor: Knute Berger	1008 Western Ave., Suite 300 Seattle, WA 98104	_____	A.M., weekly

Box 15.9 Sample List of Key Publics

LOCAL NEWSWIRE PERSONNEL

Name	Address	Editor	Phone/Fax
Associated Press News Photo Bureau	201 Boren Ave. N., Room 5 Seattle, WA 98190	John Marlow	_____
PR Newswire	1001 4th Ave., Suite 2138 Seattle, WA 98154	Derik Farley Bureau Manager	_____

Step 7: Identify the Crisis Team and Draft a Crisis Directory

Many organizations choose to place the crisis team directory near the beginning of the Crisis Communications Plan—after the cover page, introduction, and acknowledgments. Others feel that the crisis team, if rehearsed, knows its members, making this list less urgent than the list of key publics.

Regardless of where the directory appears, it should include all contact numbers, maybe even for neighbors, relatives, weekend homes, and so on. There should also be backups for each person.

See Figure 15.5 on page 109 for an example of a crisis communications team directory. Write in the names that fit your organization.

This section should also identify the spokesperson and provide tips for him or her.

Step 8: Identify the Media Spokesperson

The media spokesperson represents the company and speaks on behalf of the company. The spokesperson must be selected very carefully. In addition, two or three backup spokespersons should be selected in advance, in case the primary spokesperson is unavailable at the time of a crisis.

Criteria for Selecting

- The spokesperson must have the power to make decisions and be accessible throughout the crisis.
- The spokesperson must be articulate. He or she must be able to talk clearly, concisely, and in a pleasant manner.
- The spokesperson must appear rational, concerned, and empathetic during a crisis.
- Multiple spokespersons, when used, must all be prepared to speak in one voice, delivering the same information.

Primary and Backup	Office Phone	Cell Phone	Home Phone	E-mail
Spokespersons				
Spokesperson 1:				
Spokesperson 2:				
Spokesperson 3:				
Spokesperson 4:				

Interview Tips

- Prepare for answering who, what, when, where, why, and how questions.
- Focus on two or three key messages to communicate, and repeat them during the interview.
- Gather background information that may be useful during the interview.
- Be aware of subjects, issues, and questions that might be brought up.
- Be accessible and pleasant to reporters; show respect, and remember their names, if possible.
- Avoid saying "No comment."
- Be honest.
- Remain calm, courteous, truthful, concerned, and, if necessary, apologetic.
- Face the reporter, not the camera or microphone.
- Avoid jargon: Speak in everyday language.
- Do not speculate. Do not answer questions you don't understand. Ask for clarification.
- Be trained ahead of time, rehearsed well in advance of the crisis, and briefed prior to responding to the media.

Trick Questions (Rude Q's)

Reporters might bring you into a difficult situation by asking you trick questions. Following are examples of various types of trick question. Try to make a list of trick questions your spokesperson might be asked. Make sure he/she is prepared to answer them.

1. Speculative questions that begin with *if*:

    - "If the hamburgers that were infected were served during the normal lunch hour instead of late at night, how many people would have been infected?"
    - "If the hamburger had been cooked at a higher temperature, would the *E. coli* outbreak have happened?"

2. Leading questions:

    - "You do agree that UDUB Burger could have avoided this crisis, right?"

3. Loaded questions:

    - "Isn't it true that you knew there was an *E. coli* outbreak but couldn't do anything to stop it at once, so it caused so many deaths?"
    - "Isn't it true that you knew of possible *E. coli* in the undercooked hamburgers?"
    - "Isn't it true that you knew this employee had hepatitis A and that you failed to do anything about it?"
    - "Isn't it true that the shift manager should have been aware of the warning signs of this crisis?"

4. Naïve questions:

   - "What exactly does UDUB do?"

   - "What type of food does UDUB serve?"

5. False questions containing inaccurate details that reporters want you to correct:

   - "There were only two employees during the rush hours, right?"

   - "About 90 percent of your meat comes from the same plant that the contaminated meat from Jack-in-the-Box came from, correct?"

   - "More than seven people have been affected by the virus strain that started here at your restaurant, right?"

6. Know-it-all questions:

   - "We have all the facts. I just need to confirm a few things with you, okay?"

   - "I have all of the details, but could you give me some wrap-up comments about this crisis?"

7. Silence: This tactic aims to get you to "spill your guts."

8. Accusatory questions designed to make you blame someone else:

   - "Who is actually responsible for this crisis?"

9. Multiple-part questions designed to be intentionally confusing:

   - "What is the temperature at which you cook your meat, and is that the regulation for Washington? If it is, then how can someone contract this virus if heat is supposed to kill it?"

10. Jargon questions: Make sure to avoid using technical words that can confuse publics.

11. Chummy questions:

    - "Hey pal, off the record, why do you think this happened?"

12. Labeling questions:

    - "Would you say that the atmosphere here at UDUB Burger is 'stressful'?"

    - "Would you call the fast-paced environment stressful enough for one to lose sight of a specified task?"

13. Good-bye questions (reporters give the impression that the interview is over before asking such questions):

    - "Good-bye. Oh, by the way, how did this crisis actually happen?"

Step 9: List Emergency Personnel

Emergency personnel are usually not notified by PR personnel. They are usually part of the organization's more comprehensive crisis management plan. Often, however, if there is no larger plan, PR personnel should also plan to notify the emergency personnel. PR frequently needs emergency numbers that it can call to gather information, research damage in a crisis, and so forth.

Make charts like those for the crisis team and the media. Here is an example from UDUB Burger's Crisis Communications Plan.

Box 15.10 Sample List of Emergency Personnel

Seattle Police Department
610 3rd, Seattle 98104
911
Media Relations: 684–5520
FAX: 684–8197

Fire Department
325 2nd, Seattle 98104
911
Dept. Info: 386–1400
FAX: 386–1412

Harbor View Medical Center
325 9th Ave, S. Seattle 98104
PR: 731–4199
FAX: 731–8605

Virginia Mason
925 Seneca, Seattle 98101
Communications: 583–6082
FAX: 223–6744

UW Medical Center
1959 NE Pacific St., Seattle 98105
PR: 543–3620
FAX: 685–3333

Swedish Medical Center
PR: 386–6797
FAX: _____

Kings County Department of Health
206–269–4755

Step 10: Equipment and Supplies for the Crisis Control Room

Include in this list the person responsible for getting each item and from where. Also crucial is the site of the control room. Alternate sites are important.

During a crisis, an appointed person (usually the crisis control room coordinator) gathers supplies and materials and checks off the items on the crisis plan list. If possible, have these supplies already prepared. Some companies have rooms set aside and equipped. Supplies not listed may be pertinent to your operation.

Box 15.11 Sample List of Equipment and Supplies for the Crisis Control Room

_____ televisions (more than one to be tuned to various channels)

_____ chairs

_____ desks

_____ computers

_____ perhaps manual typewriters in case power is a problem

_____ bulletin boards

_____ flip charts

_____ computer printers

_____ telephones

_____ cellular phones

_____ battery-powered televisions and radios

_____ one or two chalkboards

_____ maps of the plant or crisis area

_____ battery-powered lamps and flashlights

_____ police radio

_____ walkie-talkies

_____ company letterhead

_____ pens

_____ pencils

_____ telephone directories

_____ contact lists

_____ media directories

_____ press kits

_____ crises plans

_____ street and highway maps

_____ food and beverages

_____ copying machine

_____ first-aid kits

_____ cameras and film

It should be noted here that, in recent crises, particularly Hurricane Katrina, tools from days gone by have been very useful. Manual typewriters are useful because they do not require electricity. For the same reason, telephones that did not require electricity lasted longer during the flooding; this means no caller I.D. or lights. Every office and every home should have at least one. Another archaic, but useful, tool is carbon paper.

Step 11: Pre-Gather Information

Prepare and gather various documents that may possibly be needed during a crisis. Keep identical sets of documents in various locales to ensure availability. Among the possibilities are these:

Box 15.12 Sample List of Pre-Gathered Information

_____ safety precautions

_____ safety records

_____ prodromes and follow-up

_____ backgrounders

_____ executive biographies

_____ annual reports

_____ photos

_____ maps of site(s)

_____ location of offices

_____ fact sheets

_____ phone books

_____ fill-in-the blanks news release

_____ Internet sources

(Also included in the Crisis Communications Plan but not shown here are a history of UDUB Burger and information on its community relations programs, employee relations programs, and so forth.)

The following five documents are samples of pre-gathered information for UDUB Burger Drive-In: a fill-in-the-blanks news release, cooking procedures, fact sheet, glossary, and Internet sources.

Box 15.13 Fill-in-the-Blanks News Release

For Immediate Release   Press Release

Date _____

POSSIBLE FOOD POISONING INCIDENT

A UDUB Burger Drive-In customer is being treated for (illness) at (hospital). (His/Her) condition is (_____). As of right now, it is unknown if (he/she) contracted (illness) at the (_____) UDUB Burger location, where (he/she) ate (when).

"We are very concerned about (victim's name) and we are monitoring (his/her) condition. Whether the illness came from food at UDUB Burger or some other source, we wish for (his/her) speedy recovery," UDUB President, Dick xxxx said.

(Victim's name) ate (what victim ate) at the UDUB Burger Drive-In (location). (Victim's name) became ill (when) after experiencing (side effects/symptoms).

Officials at UDUB Burger took immediate action to see if it is possible that the illness is a direct result of eating contaminated food at the restaurant. At this time, they have not found any evidence, but they are continuing their investigation.

There have been no reported cases of (illness) from eating at UDUB Burger in the restaurant's 45-year history.

UDUB Burger has a strict sanitary code that requires employees to cook hamburgers to 160 degrees, 10 degrees higher than required by the U.S. Food and Drug Administration (FDA). Employees are thoroughly trained in cooking, safety, and health procedures.

(*E. coli* is a bacterium that comes in many forms, most of which are harmless. Distinctive symptoms include abdominal cramps and bloody diarrhea. These symptoms appear 3 to 5 days after eating contaminated food and usually go away in 6 to 8 days. Symptoms of hepatitis A include fatigue, vomiting, jaundice, pain in the liver area, and dark urine. These symptoms can appear up to 50 days after ingesting contaminated food. There is currently no treatment for the disease, although rest and proper nutrition can relieve some symptoms.)

Box 15.14 Cooking Procedures

• UDUB Burger cooks all hamburgers to 160 degrees, which is 10 degrees higher than required by the FDA.

• UDUB Burger uses temperature-taking procedures to ensure that its hamburgers are cooked to 160 degrees.

• All employees of UDUB Burger have a food-handler permit.

• Employees are trained in cooking, safety, and health procedures

Employee safety and health information can be found in the Employee Handbook. The following two pages discuss the cooking procedures of UDUB Burger in detail. This information is from UDUB Burger Drive-Ins, Ltd.

Box 15.15 *E. coli* Fact Sheet

Definition of *E. coli*. *E. coli* is an emerging cause of food-borne illness. *E. coli* are germs (bacteria) that normally live in the intestines of people and animals. There is no treatment for *E. coli*.

What are the Symptoms?

The most common symptoms are severe stomach cramps and diarrhea. Some people vomit or run a fever, but these symptoms are less common. These symptoms usually go away by themselves after 6 to 8 days. In a small number of people, this strain of *E. coli* can cause a rare but serious problem called hemolytic uremic syndrome (HUS).

What is HUS?

HUS is a disease that affects the kidneys and blood-clotting system. In severe cases, dialysis is used for a limited time to do the kidneys' work. Some people also develop a bleeding problem or low red blood cell count (anemia).

Where is *E. coli* Found?

It lives in the intestines of healthy cattle and gets into the meat when cattle are slaughtered. The germs are killed when the meat is thoroughly cooked. Germs have also been found in raw milk, apple cider, and salami.

How is *E. coli* Spread?

E. coli must be swallowed to cause an infection. This can happen if you eat or drink something that contains these germs and that is not properly cooked or pasteurized. The germs can be spread from person to person, if someone who is infected does not thoroughly wash his or her hands with soap and water before preparing food for others.

How is *E. coli* Prevented?

Take the following steps to avoid infection:

- Do not eat non-pasteurized dairy products or undercooked ground beef.

- Do not drink raw milk or apple cider that is made from unwashed apples.

- Always wash your hands with soap and water after going to the bathroom, changing a diaper, or handling raw meat.

Box 15.16 Glossary of Food-Related Illness

Botulism: A disease caused by contamination of certain foods by the botulism bacterium commonly found in the soil. The botulism toxin is produced when the bacteria grow in improperly canned foods and occasionally in contaminated seafood. Common symptoms are headaches, nausea, vomiting, constipation, and overall weakness. It progressively attacks the nervous system, causing double vision, muscle paralysis, and difficulty with breathing and speech. Symptoms appear 8 to 12 hours after eating contaminated food. Death may occur within 3 to 7 days without treatment. There is an antitoxin to treat the disease.

Campylobacteriosis: Bacteria found in the intestinal tracts of healthy animals and untreated water surfaces. Inadequately cooked animal products and nonchlorinated water are the most common reasons for human infection. They can be easily killed by heat above 129 degrees Fahrenheit. Common symptoms are abdominal cramping, diarrhea, fever, headache, muscle pain, and nausea. Symptoms appear 2 to 5 days after eating contaminated food and may last 2 to 7 days.

Clostridium Perfringens: Bacteria found in soil, unprocessed foods, nonpotable water, and the intestinal tracts of humans and animals. It is a milder form of botulism. Symptoms include abdominal pain and diarrhea. Symptoms appear 8 to 24 hours after eating contaminated food and may last 1 to 2 days.

***E. coli* Hemolytic Colitis**: Bacteria that come in many forms; most are harmless, except the *E. coli* 0157:H7 strain. Abdominal cramps and bloody diarrhea are distinctive symptoms of this strain. Other symptoms are fever, nausea, and vomiting. These symptoms appear 3 to 5 days after eating contaminated food. Symptoms may last 10 days.

Hepatitis A Virus: A highly contagious virus that attacks the liver. The virus is transmitted by the fecal–oral route, through close person-to-person contact, or by ingesting contaminated food or water. Common symptoms are fatigue, nausea, vomiting, fever, jaundice, pain in the liver area, dark urine, and abdominal pain. The disease can stay in the body for 10 to 50 days without producing symptoms. Recovery usually takes 1 to 2 weeks.

Listeriosis: Bacteria that live in humans and animals. It is usually associated with cattle and sheep having abortions and encephalitis. The elderly, newborn babies, pregnant women, and people with a weakened immune system are the most vulnerable to this infection. Possible symptoms are fever, headaches, nausea, and vomiting. Symptoms appear 3 days to a few weeks after eating contaminated food and may last several days. Death may occur in rare cases.

Salmonellosis: Bacteria spread through contact with human or animal intestinal contents or excrement, usually found in raw meat, fish, poultry, and eggs. Symptoms, which are headache, vomiting, nausea, chills, fever, diarrhea, and abdominal cramping, appear 12 to 36 hours after eating contaminated food. The symptoms may last 2 to 7 days.

Staphylococcal Intoxication: Bacteria found on the skin and in the nose and throat of most humans. People with sinus infections and colds are high-risk carriers. Infected wounds are rich sources of this bacterium. Sewage, raw milk, and untreated water are carriers. Symptoms include vomiting, nausea, diarrhea, and abdominal cramping. Symptoms appear 1 to 8 hours after eating contaminated food and may last 1 to 2 days.

Box 15.17 Internet Sources

www.cdc.gov/ncidod/ncid.htm

National Center for Infectious Diseases (NCID) Website

- Learn about the NCID
- Disease information
- Bacterial information
- Access to *Emerging Infectious Diseases* journal

www.doh.wa.gov/Topics/ecoli.htm

Public Fact Sheet About *E. coli*

- What is it?
- Who gets it?
- How does it spread?
- What are the symptoms?
- How is it diagnosed?

www.doh.wa.gov/Topics/hepafact.html

Public Fact Sheet About Hepatitis A

- What is hepatitis A?
- How does it spread?
- How is it contracted?
- Overall history

www.jackinthebox.com

Jack-in-the-Box Website

www.ificinfo.health.org

International Food Information Council Website

www.odwalla.com

Odwalla Website

Step 12: Develop Key Messages

Messages must be tailored to each public, just as means of communication are selected for each public. The first statement made to each public sets the stage for the rest of the crisis. It establishes credibility or lack of it.

The statement to all publics should include information about the nature of the crisis, emergency, or accident; the 5 Ws and H (*what, where, when, why, who,* and *how*); the steps the organization will take to recover; and the deaths or injuries. It should also include a comment about the corporate culture.

Key messages can be drafted in advance and altered at the time of the crisis to fit the occasion. Advance preparation allows the PR professional to organize the statement carefully, without stress.

Key messages may change as the crisis develops. Examples of key messages are:

- "At the company, safety is more important than production."
- "Our employees are our first priority."

Once notification of the crisis and initial key messages have been given, strategies designed to accomplish objectives are established. Then, tactics are devised to fit the key messages, the public, and the strategy. All messages may be altered as the crisis develops.

In Box 15.18 sample key messages about *E. coli* and hepatitis A from the UDUB Burger plan are shown.

Step 13: Plan Dissemination of Key Messages

Determine the best methods of communicating key messages to key publics, including the media. Also determine who on the crisis team will be responsible for communicating to each key public.

Checklists for each branch of the news media (Figures 15.9–15.10) follow the overall plan for communications (Figure 15.6). Figures 15.7 through 15.10 are for your use.

Step 14: Update Website to Explain the Crisis

This task, in some cases, should be done prior to contacting some of the other news media. It is listed separately here because it requires the work of a webmaster, who should probably be on the crisis team, but may not be. The message should be consistent with other messages.

Step 15: Blog Responses

If there are blogs that require response, do that as soon as possible. Many organizations set up their own blogs in addition to a website.

Box 15.18 Samples of Company Position and Key Messages

E. COLI

In the event of an *E. coli* outbreak, UDUB Burger employees' first priority is the care of our customers. Warning the public of the symptoms of *E. coli* is the first order of business. The symptoms can include one or more of the following: abdominal cramps, bloody diarrhea, and nausea. Our primary concern is with those who are infected with *E. coli*. Without knowing the exact location where the *E. coli* originated, whether from the meat distributor or inside our store, we promise the public that the source of the bacteria will be discovered as promptly and effectively as possible.

We will also re-state consistently the fact that we are concerned with the *E. coli* problem and that our primary concern is for those infected. We will re-state how careful and cautious UDUB Burger is in preventing diseases such as this one from occurring. We will state that our employees cook meat to the standard temperature set by the FDA, and that employees follow proper cleaning procedures outlined by the FDA. We will explain that our employees are required to receive a food-handler permit prior to working at UDUB Burger.

The following key messages should be stressed in the order indicated:

1. Our biggest concern is for those affected.

2. We are sorry for what happened and we take full responsibility for what happened.

3. We don't know how it happened, but we are trying to find out and we'll let you know as soon as we know.

4. We maintain a strict and thorough process to avoid problems such as these from occurring by requiring our employees to receive a food-handler permit.

HEPATITIS A

In the event of a hepatitis A scare, UDUB Burger employees' first priority is the care of our customers. Warning the public of the symptoms of hepatitis A is the first order of business. The symptoms can include one or more of the following: fatigue, nausea, vomiting, fever/chill, jaundice, pain in the liver area, dark urine, light-colored stools, and/or abdominal pain. Our primary concern is with those who are infected with hepatitis A. Without knowing the exact location where the hepatitis A originated, whether from one of the employees or an external source, we promise the public that the source of the disease will be discovered as promptly and effectively as possible.

Box 15.18—continued

We will also re-state consistently the fact that we are concerned with hepatitis A and that our primary concern is for those infected. We will re-state how careful and cautious UDUB Burger is in preventing diseases such as this one from occurring. We will state that employees are required to receive a food-handler permit prior to working at UDUB Burger and that they must wash their hands before handling food.

The following key messages should be stressed in the order indicated:

1. Our biggest concern is for those affected.

2. We are sorry for what happened and we take full responsibility for what happened.

3. We don't know how it happened, but we are trying to find out and we'll let you know as soon as we know.

4. We maintain a strict and thorough process to avoid problems such as these from occurring by requiring our employees to receive a food-handler permit.

Step 16: Review Draft of the Crisis Plan and Make Corrections

Step 17: Distribute Plan to All Members of the Crisis Team

Step 18: Review and Update the Plan Once Each Year

Step 19: Drill and Rehearse Plan

Step 20: Drill and Rehearse With Spokespersons

Step 21: Evaluate the Plan

Box 15.19 shows a sample document from UDUB Burger's crisis plan.

Box 15.19 Evaluation of Plan Effectiveness After a Crisis

After a crisis, the following steps will be followed to ensure that UDUB Burger is better prepared for the future. This evaluation is for looking at what went right and what went wrong during the crisis. It covers all aspects of the crisis, including media relations, community relations, and the crisis management team performance. It is vital to evaluate the company's Crisis Communications Plan while the crisis is still fresh in employees' minds. Thinking about all aspects of the crisis will help determine what we can do better next time.

1. Media relations: Review the media's coverage of the crisis. Were there areas in which we could have received better or more positive coverage of our company? Would the coverage have been better if we had taken more time to build strong media relationships before the crisis?

2. Community relations: Did the community react favorably to how we handled the crisis? If not, what can we do to build better community relations (i.e., public service donations or activities)? If we donate money or services, make sure that the public is aware of it (through media coverage or information at our restaurant locations).

3. Crisis management team: Did all team members perform well under pressure? Were there certain members who should have been put "behind the scenes" or on the "frontlines" (speaking to the media, etc.)? Should any members be replaced by others if another crisis should occur? Was the crisis control room properly stocked? Was there anything missing that needs to be ordered or created?

Activities

Make a list of enabling publics, functional publics, normative publics, and diffused publics of your college or university—persons who would be notified in the event of a particular crisis, such as an earthquake. Remember that all contact numbers are essential: home phone, office phone, fax, e-mail, cell phone, and pager. For this exercise, however, office numbers will suffice.

- *Enabling publics:* These are the people with the power and authority to make decisions. They include the board of directors, shareholders, investors, and key executives. Notification of enabling publics should be a priority.

- *Functional publics:* These are the people who actually make the organization work: employees, unions, suppliers, vendors, consumers, and volunteers in the case of non-profit organizations.

- *Normative publics:* These are people who share values with the organization in crisis: trade associations, professional organizations, and competitors.

- *Diffused publics:* These are people with indirect links to the organization in crisis. The main diffused public is the media. Others are community groups and neighbors of the physical plant.

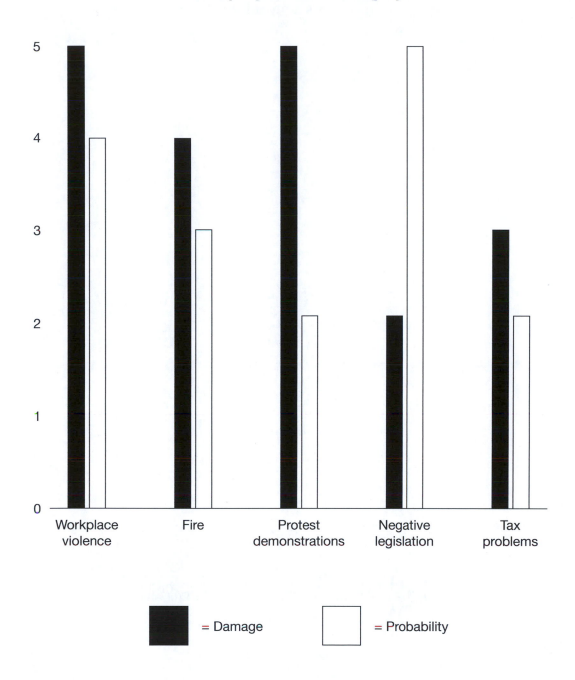

Figure 15.1 A completed sample graph of a crisis inventory.

Figure 15.2 A blank graph for plotting a crisis inventory.

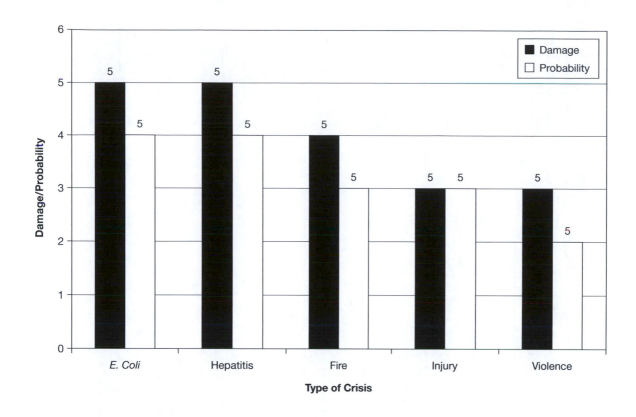

Figure 15.3 UDUB's Crisis Inventory.

LIST OF KEY PUBLICS: INTERNAL

In the event of a crisis, the following people should be informed immediately. A telephone tree should be used. The person who learns about the crisis first notifies Jim xxxx, vice president. Jim xxxx then informs the Corporate General Partner and Operations Management groups. Ken xxxx, general manager, notifies the Restaurant Operations group. The store managers then notify their employees. Lisa xxxx, director of training, notifies the Other Managers group. These managers then notify their employees.

NAME	ADDRESS	Office Phone	Cell Phone	Emergency Phone
Corporate General Partner Group				
Dick xxxx, president & co-founder				
Ina Lou xxxx, vice president & legal counsel				
Jim xxxx, vice president & legal counsel				
Walt xxxx, vice president				
John xxxx, director of technical support				
Operations Management Group				
Ken xxxx, general manager				
Lisa xxxx, director of training				
Restaurant Operations Group				
Kim xxxx, 45th Street store manager				
Bert xxxx, Broadway store manager				
Jerry xxxx, Broadway substitute store manager				
Angie xxxx, Holman Road store manager				
Paul xxxx, Queen Anne store manager				
Other Managers Group				
Jeanne xxxx, office manager				
Jodie xxxx, training manager				
John xxxx, facilities reserve manager				
Mel xxxx, facilities projects manager				

Figure 15.4 A chart similar to this should be available so that crisis notification and communication may be made.

CRISIS COMMUNICATIONS TEAM

Title	Employee	Office Phone	Cell or Car Phone	Emergency Phone	E-mail
Crisis Communications Manager *Duties:*					
Backup Crisis Communications Manager *Duties:*					
Assistant Crisis Communications Manager *Duties:*					
Crisis Control Room Coordinator *Duties:*					
Spokesperson 1 *Duties*					
Spokesperson 2 *Duties*					
Expert *Duties:*					
Print Media Contact Person *Duties:*					
TV/Radio Media Contact Person *Duties:*					
Legal Advisor *Duties:*					

Figure 15.5 A sample crisis communications team directory.

YOUR COMPANY

Message: There has been an explosion in the plant. There are injured employees. We do not know, at this time, the cause of the explosion or the extent of the injuries of the employees. An investigation is underway.

Methods of Communication

		Telephone	E-mail	Fax	Letter by Messenger	Letter by Mail	News-letter	Bulletin Board	Personal Visit	News Release	Meetings
P	Employees	*J. Nass			*J. Nass	*J. Nass					
U	Executives	*Nelson J.	*Nelson J.					*Nelson J. M. Yerina		*Nelson J.	
B	Customers				*Damian L.						
L	Board of Directors	*Nelson J.		*Damian L.				*Gina A.			
I	Electronic Media	*K. Stone		*K. Stone					*Gina A.		
C	Daily Newspapers	*Gina A.							*Gina A.		
	Weekly Newspapers		*Gina A.		*Damian L.						
S	Shareholders		*Ann C.				*Ann C.				
	Community Leaders		*Karen N.		*Karen N.						

*Staff member responsible for communications and follow-up.

Figure 15.6 A sample chart showing key publics of a fictitious organization, methods of communication, and crisis personnel responsible for the communication. The key message is written at the top of the chart. Social media networks may be used if they are favored methods of communications.

YOUR COMPANY

Message: _____

Methods of Communication

	Telephone	E-mail	Fax	Letter by Messenger	Letter by Mail	News-letter	Bulletin Board	Personal Visit	News Release	Meetings
P	*									
U										
B										
L										
I										
C										
S										

Figure 15.7 A blank chart for plotting an organization's publics, communication methods, personnel responsibilities, and key messages.

Crisis Communications Checklist

Nature of Crisis _____

Date of Occurrence _____   Time _____

Response	By Whom	Date	Time	Comments
Crisis center set up.				
Crisis team mobilized.				
Key stakeholders notified:				
CEO				
Lawyer				
Mayor				
Union officials				
Insurance agent				
_____				
_____				
Basic facts gathered.				
What happened?				
When?				
Cause?				
Number of deaths?				
Number of injuries?				
Extent of damage?				
Names/titles of deceased?				
Names/titles of injured?				
What is being done?				
Emergency officials at scene?				
Estimated return to normalcy?				
Notification of nearest of kin of deceased or injured?				
Dissemination of facts of crisis?				

Response	By Whom	Date	Time	Comments
Contact company officials				
Contact city officials				
Contact state officials				
Contact federal officials				
Contact employees				
Contact emergency officials				
Contact stockholders				
Contact board of directors				
Contact volunteers				
Contact neighbors				
Contact community leaders				
Contact competitors				
TV Station 1				
TV Station 2				
Radio News Station 1				
Radio News Station 2				
Newspaper 1				
Newspaper 2				
News Conference				

Figure 15.8 When each activity is completed, the person, date, and time are recorded. Important comments are included.

TELEVISION NEWS CHECKLIST

Station Call Letters	Channel	Address	News Director	Phone	Fax

Figure 15.9a **A blank television news checklist for filling in the contact names and numbers for all the persons whom you may have to contact at television news stations. These contacts may be on a social media network.**

RADIO NEWS CHECKLIST

Station Call Letters	Dial #	Address	News Director	Phone	Fax

Figure 15.9b A blank radio news checklist for filling in the names and numbers of radio personnel needed in a crisis. These contacts may be on a social media network.

NEWSPAPER CHECKLIST

Name of Newspaper	Who Contacted	When Contacted	Response	Circulation	Phone/Fax

Figure 15.10 A blank newspaper checklist for filling in the names of newspaper editors, reporters, and others who may have to be contacted during a crisis.

Table 15.1 Company Z's Ranking of Crisis Probability and Damage

Crisis Type	Probability	Damage
Workplace violence	4	5
Fire	3	4
Protest demonstrations	2	5
Negative legislation	5	2
Tax problems	2	3